# The Story

Growing up on a rural Minnesota farm during the 1970s and 1980s, I discovered the powerful combination of food and family. When I recall some of my fondest memories, whether they were family celebrations, holidays, summertime on the farm or at the lake, food and family tied it all together.

-Jen

## Our Farm "Crew"

Let me introduce our "crew" on the farm.
My dad, Kenneth Shelstad, grew up on the same farmstead where he later raised his own family. The farmstead was located about 20 miles southeast of Breckenridge, Minnesota.

My dad has seven siblings - four girls and three boys. He is the youngest of the boys and spent a lot of time in the kitchen with his mother and sisters. Cooking has always been important in our family. Some of the recipes featured in Minnesota Roots are handed down to me by my father's siblings.

When my dad was in his early 20s, he met my mother, Roxanne McKee, who was attending an X-ray technician program in Wahpeton, North Dakota. Wahpeton and Breckenridge are separated by the Red River which runs along the state border. My parents have been married for 60 years now.

In 1963, they had my sister, Rebecca. My brother, Eric, was born with complications during delivery a couple years later. Sadly, he was not able to live at home due to his developmental disabilities. In 1970, I was adopted as a baby and joined the crew.

*Roger, John, Carolyn, Irene, Eleanor, Marlys, and Kenneth.*

# MINNESOTA *Roots*

*Memories of family and food on our Minnesota farm with recipes curated from the Shelstad Family Collection.*

Jen Switzer & Megan Stezka

Copyright © 2023 Jen Switzer and Megan Stezka
All rights reserved. This book or any portion thereof may not be reproduced or used in any manner whatsoever without the express written permission of the publisher except for the use of brief quotations in a book review.

First printing, 2023.

The Black Hat Press
22 Broadway St SW
Isanti, MN 55040

ISBN: 978-1-7372231-5-3

www.theblackhatpress.com
@theblackhatpress

## How It All Started

My dad raised wheat, barley, corn and sugar beets on our farmland. In the early years before I came along, he also raised pigs, cows, chickens and even a few ducks. It was hard work with seemingly unending days in late summer and fall.

From spring plant through the fall harvest, Mom was the chief cook and baker. She ensured there was a hearty lunch for Dad, afternoon treats to keep his energy up on those long days and dinner on the table for the family each night.

Baking on the farm was not just for special occasions, it was a daily or weekly activity with an important purpose. Cookies, bars and cakes provided extra energy for my dad for those extended days in the tractor. My mom would deliver treats to the field if it was going to be a particularly long day. On other days, my dad would swing back to the farmhouse for a much needed break - just enough time for a cup of coffee and a sweet treat.

I first learned my way around the kitchen through baking. I now realize that I was quite fortunate to learn to cook and bake from scratch. Until I went to college, I thought that was just how everyone grew up.

Some of my friends in college baked, but when pressed for a recipe, I learned it was out of a box. Box cake definitely serves a purpose in a pinch; however, it doesn't take that much more time to bake from scratch. If you give a recipe or two from this collection a try, I think you will agree that results are worth the minimal extra effort.

In the summer months after school was out, baking provided a creative outlet for me. I had two childhood friends from our church who lived on neighboring farms. Though they were our "neighbors," their farms were not even close enough to visit by bicycle! Instead, we had weekly "play dates" arranged at one house or the other.

The other six days a week, I had to find ways to entertain myself in the summer. I read, went for bicycle rides, explored the woods surrounding the farm and I loved to bake.

Baking was a chemistry experiment with potential for a delicious outcome. It kept me fascinated. The dessert recipes included in this collection are just a few classic farmhouse favorites from back in the day that I loved to bake then, and still bake now. We have so many of these recipes in our family that we could have created a collection of just sweet treats and desserts!

As I grew older, baking evolved into a passion for cooking. When I became a young wife and mother to my own daughter, Megan, I adapted and developed my own style in the kitchen. My "Minnesota roots" provided a foundation to expand upon. I'd like to believe that I handed this foundation down to Megan.

Megan has become a brilliant and talented home chef with a passion for gardening. Her interest in learning more about our family's kitchen heritage was the spark of inspiration for this collaborative collection of recipes, memories and photographs. Megan is also an accomplished photographer based in Minneapolis, Minnesota. Her talent shows through in every photo she lovingly took of the recipes in Minnesota Roots.

## Before You Begin

Keep in mind that recipes from prior generations were more of guidelines, with personal adaptations written on notecards or scraps of paper. Many were handed down by teaching someone how to cook or bake a dish, from there it was done by rote memory.

Megan and I have worked to preserve the simple nature of the recipes that were handed down to me from our family. We have adapted where we felt it was needed, adding a little more instruction or adjusting ingredients to options that are readily available today. We wanted to keep the spirit intact while allowing you to pick the recipe up and recreate it easily.

You will also find, as Megan did while she methodically cooked and baked her way through these recipes and then photographed each one, that we often cooked or baked for a crowd. Potlucks and large family gatherings plus church social activities meant the recipes were often already scaled up to feed our large extended family or for social events at church. In most cases, you can scale back the recipes to make smaller quantities.

I hope you enjoy our trip back to the Shelstad family farm as we share our Minnesota roots through recipes, pictures and stories. As I look back now, I'm thankful for all I learned from my parents growing up on the farm. This recipe collection is my tribute and thanks to them for all they have done for me then, and still do for me now.

Jen (Shelstad) Switzer, author and recipe editor.

This cookbook started out as a pandemic project so I could continue to practice my food photography skills until it was safe to work with people again. Throughout this cookbook, you might see how I've grown using food styling techniques such as layering and color palettes. I was happy to grow creatively through this project and contribute my time and imagination into cooking — something that brings our family together.

Some of these recipes were new to me and others are classic meals and treats I remember from visiting my grandparents. I have always struggled to follow the recipes instructions. I am usually swapping ingredients or changing something, even in this cookbook. You may notice that the photos look a little different than the recipe. For example, I turned the meatloaf recipe into mini meatloafs. My personal favorites were the cheesy potatoes with ham, dill pickles, dinner rolls, and lemon bars. My mother is the main narrator in this book, but you will find a few recipe secrets from me sprinkled throughout. I tried to use local meat and produce whenever possible for these recipes. It makes a huge difference in taste and freshness.

Megan (Huizel) Stezka, photographer and recipe tester.

# Table of Contents

## BREAKFAST ON THE FARM

| | |
|---|---|
| Mom's Cinnamon Rolls | 12 |
| Fried Bread Dough | 14 |
| Overnight Ham and Egg Omelet | 16 |
| Bran Muffins | 18 |
| Sour Cream Coffee Cake | 20 |
| Vukku Church Pancakes | 23 |
| Egg Coffee | 24 |

## ENTERTAINING FAMILY-STYLE

| | |
|---|---|
| Holiday Crab Dip | 28 |
| Easy Veggie Dip | 31 |
| Creamy Dill Dip | 32 |
| Ribbon Sandwiches | 35 |
| Egg Salad Finger Sandwiches | 36 |
| Mom's Baked Beans | 39 |
| Mom's Potato Salad | 40 |
| Vodka Slush | 43 |
| Fruit Punch | 44 |
| Sherbet Punch | 47 |
| Hot Cocoa Mix | 48 |

## HEARTY SOUPS AND GREAT BIG SALADS

| | |
|---|---|
| Mom's Vegetable Beef Soup | 52 |
| Tomato Soup | 55 |
| Beer Cheese Soup | 56 |
| Mom's Chili | 59 |
| Potato Soup | 60 |
| Broccoli Supreme Salad | 63 |
| Cabbage Salad | 64 |
| Coleslaw Dressing | 67 |
| Creamy Cucumber Salad | 68 |
| Seven Layer Salad | 71 |
| Aunt Eunice's Shrimp Salad | 72 |
| Thousand Island Dressing | 75 |
| Banana Cream Salad | 76 |
| Cherry Coke Salad | 79 |

## AT OUR FARMHOUSE TABLE

| | |
|---|---|
| Aunt Carolyn's Rolls | 82 |
| Pan Fried Walleye | 85 |
| Salmon with Orange Miso Glaze | 86 |
| Chicken and Tiny Biscuits | 89 |
| Imperial Chicken | 90 |
| Loaded Vegetable Meatloaf | 93 |
| Classic Beef Pot Roast | 94 |
| Wild Rice Hotdish | 97 |
| Lasagna | 98 |
| Loose Meat Sandwiches (Sloppy Joes) | 101 |
| Cheesy Ham and Potatoes | 102 |
| Chow Mein (Chop Suey) | 105 |
| Corn-Crowned Pork Chops | 106 |
| Candied Carrots | 109 |
| Green Bean Casserole | 110 |
| Sweet Potatoes | 113 |
| Pan Gravy | 114 |
| Cheese Sauce | 117 |
| Spaghetti Sauce | 118 |
| Easy Cornbread | 121 |
| Pizza Dough | 122 |

## SWEET TREATS & BAKED GOODIES

| | |
|---|---|
| Caramelitas | 127 |
| Chocolate Brownies | 128 |
| Chocolate Icing | 131 |
| Fudge Nut Bars | 132 |
| Sweetened Condensed Milk | 135 |
| O'Henry Bars | 136 |
| Lemon Bars | 139 |
| My Favorite Chocolate Cake | 140 |
| Coconut Pecan Frosting | 143 |
| Cream Cheese Frosting | 143 |
| Easy "Yellow" Cake | 144 |
| Angel Food Cake | 147 |
| Soft Frosting | 148 |
| Applesauce Cake | 150 |
| Oatmeal Crispies | 153 |
| Peanut Butter Cookies | 154 |

Ginger Snaps 157
Mexican Wedding Cakes 151
Grandma's Pumpkin Cookies 161
White Rolled Cookies & Frosting 162

## HOMESTYLE DESSERTS

Crisp - Apple or Rhubarb 166
Easy Roll Pie Crust 169
Lemon Meringue Pie 170
Meringue 170
Banana Cream Pie 173
Pumpkin Pie 174
Blueberry Pie 177
Shortcake with Peaches 178
Strawberry Yogurt Dessert 181
Banana Split Frozen Dessert 182
Maple Walnut Ice Cream 185
Grandma McKee's Lemon Bread 186
Banana Bread 189
Pumpkin Bread 190
Aunt Karyn's Turtles 193

## PRESERVING IT: CANNING & FREEZING

Canning - The Basics 196
Canning Fruit 199
Pickles with Dill and Garlic 203
Making Jelly - The Basics 204
Wild Plum Jam 206
Apple Butter 209
Freezing - The Basics 210
Creamed Sweet Corn 213
Rhubarb Sauce 214
Spiced Crab Apple "Pickles" 217

## BIOGRAPHY 219

## ACKNOWLEDGEMENTS 220

*Breakfast on the Farm*

Weekday breakfasts on the farm consisted of either eggs and toast with bacon, or sausage or a bowl of cereal. Mom would stock the pantry with Raisin Brain, Grape-Nuts, Cheerios, Rice Krispies and Wheaties. You would not find a box of sugar cereal in the farmhouse pantry. Why? We could add our own, as much or as little as you wanted! Afterall, my dad raised sugar beets.

I loved to stay "in town" with our Aunt Carolyn at their Breckenridge home for storm days. Living in a rural Minnesota farming community, a surprise winter blizzard would either send us home early from school to avoid the risk of the buses getting stuck on country roads, or we would be sent to our storm homes. Everyone who lived outside of town had a designated storm home. Our storm home was our Aunt Carolyn and her husband, Reynold Ellingson's house. Carolyn is my dad's sister, the youngest of the seven.

Breakfast at Aunt Carolyn's was a special treat for me because we would have our choice of sugar cereal! My favorites were Lucky Charms or Fruity Pebbles. For a young farm girl, storm days were like vacation. Aunt Carolyn would sometimes make fried bread dough for breakfast if she happened to have extra dough left from making bread or rolls. She would turn the leftover dough into this delicious breakfast treat. To this day, the thought of fried bread dough makes me hungry and takes me right back to her kitchen.

Breakfast on the Farm includes recipes from my family's collection such as our church pancakes and my mom's cinnamon rolls, which are made in the mixer. These recipes are perfect for a tasty farm-style breakfast or brunch, whether you are feeding a crowd or just a few. Many of them are also great make-ahead recipes.

*Matthew (Rebecca's son) and Megan going for a tractor ride on the Super "C" with grandpa.*

# MOM'S CINNAMON ROLLS

*serves 12*

There is nothing like fresh baked cinnamon rolls drizzled with frosting for breakfast in the morning! Mom always served these delightful cinnamon rolls topped with a simple frosting of powdered sugar and a bit of milk. The fragrant smell of cinnamon would draw us into the kitchen to sample a roll from the very first batch.

Later, as a young mom, I loved to watch how much Megan enjoyed them when we visited my parent's lake home on Ottertail Lake. I would look on as she devoured her roll for breakfast while I sat around the kitchen table drinking coffee and talking about life with my dad.

I really like caramel rolls. Cinnamon rolls are wonderful, but a caramel bottom ensures there is a bit of gooey, sticky goodness to go with each bite of soft cinnamon bread. I have included the ingredients to adapt this recipe if you like them extra gooey like me.

---

1 ¼ ounce-package of yeast (or 2 ¼ teaspoons) mixed with ¼ cup warm water
¼ cup dry milk powder
1 cup water
¼ cup sugar
½ tablespoon salt
1 large egg
2 cups flour
¼ cup margarine
1 ½ cups flour
½ cup of butter, melted
2 cups brown sugar
1 ½ tablespoons cinnamon

1. Using an egg whip or whisk, combine yeast and warm water in a small bowl.
2. In the bowl of your stand mixer with a regular beater attachment, beat together powdered milk, water and sugar. Add salt. Mix to combine.
3. Switch to a dough hook, add in the egg and yeast mixture. Then add 2 cups of flour. Whip hard. Add margarine and remaining flour. Stir.
4. Let sit for 20 minutes. Knead on Speed 2.
5. Transfer the dough to a lightly greased mixing bowl. Cover with a towel and let rise until doubled in size, about 1 hour.
6. Preheat oven to 350°F.
7. Lightly grease a baking sheet. Punch down the dough and roll into a rectangle.
8. Brush dough with ½ cup melted butter. In a small bowl, combine brown sugar and cinnamon. Sprinkle on top of the melted butter.
9. Roll up tightly lengthwise so you have one long roll. Using a sharp serrated knife to cut the dough into twelve 1-inch slices.
10. Place the slices onto a lightly greased 9x13-inch pan.
11. Cover and let rise for 30-45 minutes.
12. Bake at 350°F for 13-15 minutes.

*Tidbits from Jen's Kitchen*

Mom's base dough recipe can also be made into a batch of soft and tender buns or finger rolls.

**Variation: Caramel Sauce for Caramel Rolls**

1 cup packed brown sugar
½ cup butter or margarine
3 tablespoons whipping cream
¾ cup pecan halves, if desired

1. In a saucepan, heat brown sugar and butter, stirring constantly until sugar is dissolved.
2. Remove from heat. Stir in whipping cream.
3. Return to heat and bring just to a boil. Remove from heat. Cool for 5 minutes.
4. Grease bottom and sides of 9x13-inch pan. Pour caramel mixture evenly over bottom of pan. Sprinkle with pecans. Top with cut cinnamon rolls.
5. Bake for at 350°F for 13-15 minutes.

# FRIED BREAD DOUGH

*serves 8*

Thoughts of winter blizzards bring back memories of storm days at Aunt Carolyn's in Breckenridge, Minnesota. One year, my dad even had to pick me up at Aunt Carolyn's on his John Deer snowmobile! It was the only way to get into town and then back to the farm. Minnesota blizzards are no joke!

Snow storms and storm days also bring back fond memories of fried bread dough at Aunt Carolyn's. She would make fried bread dough with the extra dough from baking bread or rolls. She served it with butter and maple syrup. If you sprinkle a little powdered sugar on top, you have heavenly, slightly sinful breakfast.

If you don't have leftover dough like she did, you can whip up this recipe any day of the week. It's a close second to Aunt Carolyn's and has been adapted from a recipe I discovered from King Arthur's Flour.

---

2 cups flour
2 teaspoons baking powder
¾ teaspoon salt
2 tablespoons cold, unsalted butter, cut in ½-inch cubes
¾ cup room temperature water
vegetable oil
butter
maple syrup
powdered sugar

1. Preheat oven to 200°F.
2. Mix the flour, baking powder, and salt in a medium mixing bowl to combine. Cut in cold butter using a pastry blender. Stir in water to make a dough.
3. Cover and let rest for 15 minutes.
4. Divide the dough into eight pieces. One piece at a time, roll into thin 4-5-inch rounds, no more than ½-inch thick.
5. Add vegetable oil to a frying pan, enough to not quite cover the disks of dough when placed into the oil. Heat to medium to medium-high heat.
6. Use tongs to pick up a round and carefully lower into the oil. It should sizzle. If not, your oil is not ready. Let each round fry for about 1 minute. The dough will puff up and be lightly golden brown on the bottom.
7. Flip it over and cook until the other side is lightly golden brown, about 1 more minute. Do not overcook.
8. Remove from the oil and set on a paper towel-lined cookie sheet. Place in the 200°F oven to keep warm.
9. Repeat with remaining rounds of dough.
10. Serve topped with butter, maple syrup, and sprinkled powdered sugar.

BREAKFAST ON THE FARM

# OVERNIGHT HAM AND EGG OMLET

*serves 10*

Weekday mornings often started with eggs, bacon and toast. My dad makes the best over-easy eggs. Perhaps it is the many years of practice or his ability to flip the eggs at just the right time.

Making eggs for a crowd called for another solution. It is hard to cook fried or scrambled eggs for a large motley crew like the Shelstad family. Overnight family gatherings called for easy, make-ahead breakfast options that could feed everyone. This recipe is one that Mom prepared when she needed to feed a crowd or for a holiday brunch.

The majority of our produce in the summer months came from our garden - fresh in-season or frozen for the winter. Beyond lettuce and cabbage, I don't recall that we purchased much produce from the grocery store. The rest of our produce was canned pantry staples like mushrooms. I remember leaving for college and discovering the fact that canned mushrooms were not even close to the same as fresh mushrooms. I highly recommend using fresh and not canned in this recipe.

1. Grease a 9x13-inch pan.
2. Layer 6 slices of bread on the bottom, then layer with ham, cheese and mushrooms. Repeat, ending with a layer of cheese.
3. Mix the milk, eggs, dry mustard, Worcestershire sauce and salt in a blender. Pour slowly over the bread mixture in the pan.
4. Cover with tin foil and refrigerate overnight.
5. Preheat oven to 325°F.
6. Bake for 1 hour (or more), uncovered. Baking time will depend on the type of bread you used and your oven.
7. Let stand 15 minutes before serving.

8-12 slices bread - cut off crust (if desired) and butter on both sides
2-3 cups diced ham
1 pound Swiss cheese, shredded
2 4-ounce cans of sliced mushrooms (or 1 8-ounce container of sliced fresh mushrooms)
2 cups milk
4 large eggs
2 teaspoons dry mustard
1 teaspoon Worcestershire sauce
dash salt

**Tidbits from Jen's Kitchen**

You can swap the canned mushrooms with fresh sliced cremini for a modern twist.
Opt for a bakery loaf of sourdough or other rustic bread. I love to leave the crust on a rustic sourdough for extra texture and flavor.
Not a fan of ham? You can swap out the ham for pre-cooked and cooled Italian sausage, ground beef or turkey.

BREAKFAST ON THE FARM

# BRAN MUFFINS

*serves 48*

This bran muffin recipe was from my cousin Joan. Joan is Aunt Carolyn's only daughter and the oldest of her three children. The recipe makes a large batch of tasty muffins. I bake a batch of these muffins every few months. They are one of my husband Jamie's favorite breakfasts.

---

2 cups All-Bran 100% whole bran cereal
2 cups water, boiling
1 cup shortening or vegetable oil
3 cups sugar
4 large eggs
1 quart buttermilk
5 cups flour
5 teaspoons baking soda
1 teaspoon salt
4 cups All-Bran bran flakes

1. Preheat oven to 400°F.
2. In a large mixing bowl, pour boiling water over whole bran cereal and set aside.
3. Cream shortening, sugar and eggs in another large bowl or with your mixer.
4. In a small bowl, combine flour, baking soda and salt and stir to combine.
5. Add buttermilk and flour mixture slowly to the creamed sugar, alternating between buttermilk and flour mixture, stirring to combine.
6. Once the buttermilk and flour have been incorporated, stir bran flakes into the batter, just until combined. Do not over mix.
7. Scoop into muffin pan (option to line with paper baking cups) and bake at 400°F for 15-25 minutes or until golden brown.

### Tidbits from Jen's Kitchen

All-Bran whole bran and bran flake cereals can be hard to find nowadays. I use Raisin Bran for the bran flakes and Grape Nuts for the whole bran cereal.

This recipe can be prepared in advance and refrigerated until morning. Extra batter will also keep for several days in the refrigerator. Or, as I do, bake up all four dozen and freeze half of them.

BREAKFAST ON THE FARM

# SOUR CREAM COFFEE CAKE

*serves 12*

Sour cream coffee cake is both a special treat for breakfast and a delicious dessert. Mom and I have not been able to locate our original family recipe after years of searching. It seems to have sadly disappeared! We will keep searching, and hopefully, it will turn up.

In the meantime, I needed to fill that void. After all, this was the only cake we were allowed to eat for breakfast! For this recipe, I melded together a few recipes that were "close but not quite" into something that I feel is very close.

My husband Jamie, who was born and raised in Ontario, Canada, also grew up with coffee cake. It is still a favorite. Although he has not had my childhood version, this recipe has become one of his most requested recipes. It never lasts very long when I bake it.

---

½ cup butter, softened
½ cup shortening
1 cup sugar
3 eggs, large
1 cup sour cream
2 ½ cups flour
1 tablespoon flour
2 teaspoons baking powder
1 teaspoon baking soda
⅛ teaspoon salt
1 teaspoon vanilla extract
1 teaspoon lemon extract

Topping:
1 cup pecans, chopped
2 teaspoons ground cinnamon
1 cup brown sugar
½ cup butter, melted

1. Preheat oven to 350 F. Spray a 9 x 13-inch baking pan with nonstick baking spray and then flour; set aside.
2. In a large bowl, beat butter and shortening at medium-high speed with a hand-held electric mixer until creamy, about 2 minutes.
3. Gradually add sugar, and continue to beat until light and fluffy, about 3 minutes.
4. In a small bowl, whisk together eggs and sour cream. In another bowl, whisk together 2 ½ cups flour, baking powder, baking soda, and salt.
5. Add the flour and sour cream mixtures to the butter mixture, alternating between the flour and the sour cream mixture. Begin and end with the flour mixture, beating at low speed just until combined. Stir in extracts.
6. Spread batter into a prepared pan.
7. In a small bowl, combine brown sugar, remaining 1 tablespoon flour, and cinnamon. Add brown sugar and pecans and stir to combine. Sprinkle the brown sugar topping over batter.
8. Bake until a wooden pick inserted into center comes out clean, about 45 minutes. Let cool completely in pan on a wire rack.

**Tidbits from Jen's Kitchen**

Ultimately, the original recipe was located while we were editing this cookbook. A copy had made its way to Oregon and my sister Rebecca's recipe box! My version is actually quite close to the original. The main differences are increasing the amount of cinnamon in the topping to 4 teaspoons, the use of sour cream instead of milk and the addition of lemon extract. Now that I have discovered sour cream is a baking ingredient, I am leaving my recipe well enough alone. Feel free to adjust the level of cinnamon to your taste, anywhere from 2 to 4 teaspoons.

BREAKFAST ON THE FARM

# VUKKU CHURCH PANCAKES *serves 12*

   This pancake recipe is from our rural family church, Vukku, just south of Foxhome, Minnesota. The church had an annual pancake breakfast fundraiser hosted by the men in our congregation for many years.

   Back then, you didn't find men in the kitchen very often. I still have the mental image of these men in the church basement kitchen flipping pancakes and making bacon. It always smelled and tasted amazing, but I would not want to have to clean up after them!

   I love to make this recipe when we have overnight guests and I want to whip up a big, hearty breakfast. The pancakes are light and fluffy. They are just plain good!

---

1. Stir all ingredients together in a large mixing bowl until just combined. Do not over mix.
2. Pour batter into a large pitcher.
3. Spray a griddle or skillet with non-stick cooking spray. Preheat over medium to medium-high heat. Pour batter into circles onto the griddle.
4. When the pancake(s) has formed edges and start to bubble, slide a thin spatula underneath and peek to see if it is golden brown on the bottom. Flip the pancake and cook for 1-2 minutes more, until the other side is golden brown.
5. Serve immediately with butter and maple syrup.
6. Repeat with remaining batter.

**2 teaspoons sugar**
**2 teaspoons baking soda**
**1 teaspoon salt**
**3 teaspoons baking powder**
**4 eggs**
**¼ cup combination of butter and lard (2 tablespoons each)**
**4 cups buttermilk**
**3-4 cups flour (just enough flour that it flows easily from a pitcher)**
**butter**
**maple syrup**

### Tidbits from Jen's Kitchen

   Believe it or not the recipe has already been scaled down from the original recipe. You can scale it down even further to make just the amount you need. Pancakes freeze well so you can make the entire batch, let them cool and then freeze for another day when you need a quick breakfast. Toss a couple of frozen pancakes in the toaster to warm for a quick breakfast.

BREAKFAST ON THE FARM

# EGG COFFEE
*serves 8-10*

    Growing up in a Lutheran church, we had many social events. There were the women's quilting days, the chicken supper and the pancake breakfast to name a few. No matter the time of day or the event, coffee was always served. In the early days, egg coffee was prepared in huge enamel coffee pots in the church's kitchen.

    This style of brewing coffee was brought to Minnesota from Sweden. In the Midwest, it is often referred to as "church basement coffee" for the large quantity it usually makes. Egg coffee mixes a cracked egg into the coffee grounds before adding the grounds to boiling water. The egg helps clarify the coffee and allows the grounds to separate from the water. The egg white aids in removing the bitterness from the grounds, enhancing the caffeine. The result? A light coffee brewed with no bitterness or acidity with a smooth texture that is easy to drink. The longer it simmers the stronger the coffee is without growing bitter. And let me tell you, the Lutherans I know like strong coffee.

---

**10 ¼ cups water, divided**
**¾ cup medium to coarse ground coffee (freshly ground is the best)**
**1 large egg**
**1 cup cold water**

1. Bring 9 cups of water to a rapid boil in a saucepan or enamel coffee pot.
2. Stir the ground coffee, ¼ cup water, and a cracked egg together in a small bowl. You can also add the crushed eggshells into the coffee ground mixture as they did traditionally.
3. When the water boils, carefully pour in the egg and coffee mixture. Turn down the heat, if necessary, to prevent it from boiling over. Boil for 3 minutes or until the coffee grounds bind together and float to the top.
4. Remove from heat and pour in 1 cup cold water.
5. Let the coffee sit for 10 minutes. The grounds will settle to the bottom of the pot.
6. Pour the coffee through a fine-meshed sieve. Return to the stove to simmer, if desired. The flavor grows stronger the longer it simmers. If serving immediately, pour into a coffee carafe.

*Tidbits from Jen's Kitchen*

This is a great technique to use if you are camping or have water that is not the best for brewing coffee.

*Entertaining Family Style*

As I mentioned, my dad is the second youngest of seven siblings - four sisters and two brothers. Only one of his siblings moved out of state, my dad's sister, Eleanor Burgett. She moved to New York with her husband, Bill. They lived in New York for as long as I can remember. The rest of Dad's siblings all lived a short drive away, from Fosston in northwestern Minnesota to Kenyon in southeastern Minnesota.

By the time I was born, all my dad's siblings were married and raising their own families. I was the youngest of over 20 cousins. All this to say, when our extended family gathered for the holidays or special events like graduations and weddings, you were almost always planning for 30 plus people!

Appetizers and party foods were not fancy hor d'oeuvres. They were potluck-friendly recipes scaled up to feed a crowd. Our Uncle John and Aunt Norma Shelstad would host big New Year gatherings for the entire family when we were young. They lived on a farmstead near Kenyon, Minnesota.

The farmhouse seemed like a mansion to me as a youngster. The "mansion" was large enough to comfortably raise their seven children. And, it was also perfect for hosting the Shelstad clan! There was always lots of food devoured and tons of fun with the cousins. I remember each bedroom would be assigned to each aunt and uncle with names posted over the door. Sleeping bags would be scattered everywhere for us young ones. And then there were the Shelstad good-byes. You needed to plan for a least a couple hours of good-byes before hitting the road for the long drive home. Good memories!

Megan and I did find a couple recipes from my trusty old recipe box that are a bit more "fancy", like Aunt Marlys Jackson's ribbon sandwiches. Even these recipes were still designed to entertain family-style.

Next time you are entertaining family-style with friends or family pull out one of these tried and true classic recipes from the Shelstad collection.

*Entertaining family style at Uncle Roger's. The kitchen was a popular space for all family gatherings.*

# HOLIDAY CRAB DIP

*serves 8*

This dish was a holiday tradition for Christmas evening at the Shelstad farm. It brings back memories of attending Christmas Eve service and then returning to the farmhouse to snack on this crab dip with other snacks like cheese, crackers and herring while Mom wrapped the last of the presents.

The last of the presents were usually for me because I had already wrapped the rest. I loved to wrap presents! I think it was because I enjoyed using lots of tape so that they were harder to open or at least difficult for anyone to attempt to peek! One year for Christmas, I was even gifted a few rolls of tape as a joke.

An appetizer recipe doesn't get much easier than this crab dip. The combination of the cream cheese, cocktail sauce, and the onions is not only festive, it is downright delicious. The tangy cocktail sauce along with the slightly sweet cream cheese complements the crab while the green onion gives it a fresh burst of flavor and a little crunch.

---

**1 8-ounce package of cream cheese**
**1 12-ounce bottle of cocktail sauce, (preferably Bookbinder or Cross & Blackwell)**
**1 bunch green onions, chopped**
**1 6-8-ounce package or can of lump crab meat**

1. Spread cream cheese on the bottom of a 10-inch plate. Top with cocktail sauce and coat the cream cheese evenly with sauce.
2. Rinse crab in a strainer and press out any excess water. Pick through the crab to ensure there are no remaining shells.
3. Sprinkle crab over the cocktail sauce and then top with the green onions. Refrigerate several hours or overnight. Serve with crackers.

**Megan's Recipe Secret:**

Imitation crab or salad shrimp work well as a stand-in if lump crab meat is not readily available.

**Megan's Recipe Secret:**

Fresh is always best. I substitute fresh spinach for frozen. Just steam or saute'. Be sure to squeeze dry!

# IRENE'S EASY VEGGIE DIP

*makes 3 cups*

Veggies and dip were served at just about every family gathering, especially at the lake during the summer. This recipe is from Irene Henjum, one of my dad's older sisters. It comes together quickly and the water chestnuts give it a nice crunch.

---

1. Squeeze the spinach and remove as much excess water as you can to prevent the dip from becoming too thin.
2. Mix all ingredients together in a medium size bowl. Refrigerate for several hours or overnight.
3. Serve with veggies or crackers.

1 0.9-ounce envelope vegetable soup mix
1 10-ounce package of frozen spinach, thawed, excess water squeezed out and chopped
1 cup mayonnaise
1 cup sour cream
1 8-ounce can water chestnuts, drained and chopped
1 tablespoon chopped green onions

**Tidbits from Jen's Kitchen**

If you are not a fan of sour cream, you can substitute Greek yogurt or kefir, as I do, which adds a bit more tang than sour cream does.

ENTERTAINING FAMILY STYLE

# CREAMY DILL DIP

*makes 2 cups*

This is a quick and easy dip. It is so much better than store bought! You can serve it with vegetables or as dip for potato chips.

---

1 cup Miracle Whip salad dressing
1 cup sour cream
1 tablespoon seasoned salt
1 tablespoon dried minced onion
1 tablespoon dill weed
1 tablespoon dried parsley flakes
1 tablespoon Accent seasoning blend (or use the blend in Tidbits from Jen's Kitchen)

1. Combine all ingredients in a bowl and mix well.
2. Refrigerate for 24 hours.
3. Serve with raw vegetables or chips for dipping.

### Tidbits from Jen's Kitchen

The original family recipe calls for Accent, which is a seasoning blend that is primarily MSG (monosodium glutamate). I have discovered I am allergic to MSG. I leave it out of all my recipes. Instead of Accent you can substitute 1 teaspoon of salt, ½ teaspoon each of garlic powder, oregano and cumin and a pinch of chili powder and paprika.

ENTERTAINING FAMILY STYLE

**Megan's Recipe Secret:**

If you are not a fan of Miracle Whip like me, substitute mayo. I also like to go heavy on the sour cream and use fresh dill for this recipe.

# RIBBON SANDWICHES

*makes 12-18*

Ribbon sandwiches may have been the fanciest appetizer I remember from my childhood. You knew they were a labor of love. There was something special about those pretty layers. The combination of flavors blended so well together creating a slightly salty but yet creamy bite of goodness.

Spam is a Minnesota invention from the town of Austin. George A. Hormel founded his meatpacking facility there in 1891. Spam is that canned meat you may have seen in the store but were likely not brave enough to try. It was first produced during the Great Depression as a way for Hormel to sell its unprofitable pork shoulders. Spam became a global product during World War II, when it was shipped over to the Pacific as an inexpensive meal for our U.S. troops. It still remains popular in places like Hawaii where soldiers were stationed during war times.

---

1. Line a cookie sheet with wax paper.
2. Slice each loaf of bread into 4 sections lengthwise (the opposite direction that bread is normally sliced). It is easiest if you slice each loaf lengthwise in half and then half each section again.
3. Start with a layer of white bread on the lined cookie sheet. Layer as follows:
   - cottage cheese
   - sprinkle with parsley
   - wheat bread
   - ground ham mixed with green peppers
   - white bread
   - shredded cheddar cheese
   - wheat bread
4. Thin the cream cheese with milk. Use enough milk to allow the cream cheese to spread easily. Frost the entire layered loaf with cream cheese mixture.
5. Freeze for 30 minutes to 45 minutes until firm.
6. *Place a damp dish cloth over the sandwich loaf. Wrap the bread loaf topped cookie sheet with plastic wrap. Refrigerate or freeze until 2 hours before serving.
7. Cut widthwise (like a normal loaf of bread) into ½-inch slices.

**1 loaf of unsliced artisan white bread**
**1 loaf of unsliced artisan wheat bread**
**cottage cheese**
**1 bunch of parsley, finely minced**
**1 12-ounce can of Spam ham, finely chopped**
**1 green pepper, minced**
**1 8-ounce block of Cheddar cheese, shredded**
**1 8-ounce package of cream cheese, softened**
**milk, to thin**

### Tidbits from Jen's Kitchen

If you are not brave enough to try Spam, you can use ground ham, pepperoni or salami. Or, you substitute the meat layer for a vegetable layer of finely diced roasted red peppers, cream cheese and perhaps a bit of fresh basil.

*Non-stick tin foil is now available and it is a much easier option than the damp towel and plastic wrap method in the original recipe. This is one modern convenience I would opt for when making this recipe.

ENTERTAINING FAMILY STYLE

# EGG SALAD FINGER SANDWICHES

*serves 8-10*

I thought tea sandwiches (also referred to as finger sandwiches in Minnesota) were so special! They were often served at women's church social events like bible studies, weddings and baby showers. This is Aunt Marlys Jackson's recipe and like many recipes from that era, is written in the form of guidance and not as detailed as modern day recipes. The egg salad instructions were simply to combine hard boiled eggs with mayonnaise, mustard and onion. We thought you may want more specific instructions. Below both a classic egg salad along with a modern day update, an avocado egg salad.

---

**1 caraway, whole wheat, or cocktail bread loaf (sliced ¼ inch thick)**
**butter**
**egg salad (classic or avocado)**
**1-2 cucumbers, sliced 1/8-inch thick (select small narrow cucumbers, preferably English)**

1. Gently mix all ingredients together in a bowl until mixed but still chunky.
2. Butter bread slices.
3. Top half of the bread slices with egg salad, a cucumber and top with the second slice.
4. Refrigerate until ready to serve.

*Tidbits from Jen's Kitchen*
I love both of these recipes! One is classic, one is modern. In either case, combine all the ingredients in a medium bowl and stir gently to combine.

Option 1: Classic Egg Salad
8 hard boiled eggs, chopped
¼ cup of mayonnaise
1 tablespoon minced onions
2 tablespoons dijon mustard
½ teaspoon salt
¼ teaspoon white pepper

Option 2: Avocado Egg Salad
¼ - ½ cup mashed avocado
8 hard boiled eggs, chopped
1 teaspoon dijon mustard
1 tablespoon champagne vinegar
1 tablespoon minced onion
¼ teaspoon garlic powder
¼ teaspoon salt
1 teaspoon fresh dill, for garnish

**Megan's Recipe Secret:**

Tea and finger sandwiches are small, cute little sandwiches, sometimes cut into shapes like hearts or triangles to serve at gatherings. For a simple weekday lunch, you can do as I did, turning this recipe into a traditional egg salad sandwich. Serve it on hearty multigrain bread topped with lettuce.

**Megan's Recipe Secret:**

If you have an electric pressure cooker, you can skip soaking the beans. Use a 1:3.5 ratio of beans to water. Pressure cook for 30 minutes with 15 minutes of natural release.

# MOM'S BAKED BEANS
*serves 16*

Baked beans were Mom's go-to recipe for family gatherings and potlucks. They can be prepared in advance and serve a crowd! Mom's version of baked beans is not overly saucy nor is it too sweet. It really lets the flavor of the beans take center stage.

Mom would make her beans in a large Dutch oven. When it was time to take them on the road, she would lay out a large flour sack towel on the table and place a potholder or two in the center with the Dutch oven on top. She would then pull the edges of the towel to the center and tie the ends of the towels together over the lid. The beans were now travel ready and nearly spill proof! I still pull out this handy trick when bringing a warm dish to a potluck event with friends.

We had a classic Crockpot slow cooker that Mom would use from time to time. Ours was a rusty reddish orange color and the insert was not yet removable. Once you boil the beans you can place them along with all the remaining ingredients in your slower cooker and cook all day on low. Or, use your slow cooker to reheat the beans, if prepared in advance.

---

1. Preheat oven to 350°F.
2. Rinse beans in a colander using cold water for about 1-2 minutes. Place the beans in a large Dutch oven and cover with water. Soak the beans overnight.
3. Keep beans in soaking water. Bring to a boil with ½ teaspoon baking soda. Boil for 5-10 minutes. Drain water off and rinse using a colander.
4. Return beans to the Dutch oven and add 4 cups of hot water to cover the beans. Simmer until the skins pop, about 1 hour. Don't stir.
5. Add remaining ingredients and stir gently just enough to combine.
6. Bake at 350°F for 1 ½ hours. Decrease heat to 325°F and bake for an additional 2-2 ½ hours. Alternatively, you can bake at 225°F for 11 hours.

**2 pounds white beans (dry), rinsed & drained, covered in water to soak**

**4 cups hot water (enough to cover the beans generously)**

**½ teaspoon baking soda**

**1 pound cooked bacon or ham bone**

**1-2 teaspoon salt, to taste (omit with ham bone)**

**1-2 teaspoon dry mustard powder**

**1 medium onion, chopped**

**3-6 tablespoons molasses**

**3-6 tablespoons brown sugar**

***Tidbits from Jen's Kitchen***

My mom liked her beans a little bit more salty and sweet than I do. I like to cut back the salt to 1 teaspoon and the molasses and brown sugar to 3 tablespoons.

ENTERTAINING FAMILY STYLE

# MOM'S POTATO SALAD

*serves 24*

Potato salad is a Midwestern classic. This is my mom's recipe. It was always a hit at gatherings with its creamy dressing. The recipe makes a gallon, so it is plenty to feed a crowd! I have to admit, I still struggle cooking for two or three, after learning to cook on the farm. Somehow, no matter how hard I try, I still end up making enough to feed a crowd. Just ask my husband, Jamie, he will confirm this ongoing struggle.

When I moved south, I discovered there are quite a few variations of potato salad from state to state, each with their signature regional twist. In Minnesota, Miracle Whip was the go-to base for the dressing instead of mayonnaise. Down south, Miracle Whip is not considered mayonnaise, merely a salad dressing. Mayonnaise is Duke's or Hellman's. I don't recommend you suggest that they are interchangeable to anyone who was raised in the south.

Our family's potato salad also does not include pickle relish, which may be more of a southern tradition. What sets my mom's apart from others is the hint of sugar and the addition of milk, which results in a creamy dressing that coats the potatoes ever so evenly.

Lastly, I will warn you that there is a lot of onion in my mom's recipe! You can start with one onion and decide from there how much onion flavor you like. Both my parents love onions. They believe a salad is not a salad unless it is loaded with onions.

---

**9 cups diced, cooked potatoes**
**12 large hard-boiled eggs, chopped**
**2 large onions, chopped (3 cups)**
**2 cups Miracle Whip salad dressing (or mayonnaise)**
**4 ½ tablespoons vinegar**
**4 ½ tablespoons sugar**
**12 tablespoons milk**
**2 tablespoons yellow mustard**
**salt, to taste**
**pepper, to taste**
**paprika, for garnish**

1. Boil potatoes with the skins on. Cool. Peel and dice into evenly sized cubes.
2. Ensure all ingredients are cold before combining.
3. Combine in a bowl all ingredients. Best if refrigerated overnight.

**Megan's Recipe Secret:**

I dislike both Miracle Whip and yellow mustard. For my fresh take, substitute 1 cup of your favorite oil-based vinaigrette (such as Italian) for vinegar, replace the Miracle Whip with 1 cup mayonnaise, and swap the 2 tablespoons of yellow mustard for dijon mustard. Skip the sugar and the milk. I also like to add an extra punch of flavor by adding minced fresh flat leaf parsley to the mix.

**Megan's Recipe Secret:**

I used lime-flavored sparkling water instead of soda as the juice concentrate is already sweet. I also used a peach herbal tea instead of green tea. Super yummy!

# VODKA SLUSH

*serves 25*

This recipe is from Aunt Eunice Shelstad. Eunice is married to Roger Shelstad, one of my dad's brothers. They are my godparents and their sons, Chad and David, are just a year and two years older than I. We spent a lot of time together, our two families, over the years. There are lots of great memories of these times -- playing cards, fireworks at the lake and weekends swimming and goofing around at the Sunwood Inn in Morris, Minnesota.

This slush is a refreshing and fun party cocktail that you can make ahead. It was, and is, perfect for those hot summer days at the lake or the beach. Us "kids" had our own pail that didn't have vodka...

Growing up in the Midwest, we called carbonated beverages "pop" or "soda pop." On my first trip down south in my early 20s I discovered a new regional variation. We were in New Orleans grabbing a quick bite to eat and I ordered a Coke. Imagine my surprise when the server asked me what flavor of "coke" I wanted with my meal. I was so confused! I just wanted a Coke "coke"! Asking for a coke in New Orleans is like asking for a kleenex instead of a tissue.

---

1. Bring 7 cups of water and sugar to a boil. Set aside and cool.
2. Boil remaining 2 cups of water and add tea bags. Allow tea bags to steep while it cools.
3. Mix all ingredients, except lime-lime soda, in a large ice cream pail or other freezer-safe container with a lid. Put it in the freezer overnight or longer.
4. To Serve: Fill a glass half full of slush and top with lemon-lime pop, orange pop, sour or club soda.

**9 cups water, divided**
**2-3 cups sugar**
**4 green tea bags**
**1 12-ounce can lemonade concentrate**
**1 12-ounce can orange juice concentrate**
**2 cups vodka**
**lemon-lime or orange "pop," sour mix or club soda, to finish**

ENTERTAINING FAMILY STYLE

# FRUIT PUNCH

*serves 16*

Big celebrations like graduations and weddings called for breaking out the punch bowl, making an ice ring and whipping up a big batch of punch. This was the go-to recipe for punch at our family celebrations.

---

**2 3-ounce packages Jell-O, cherry, strawberry or raspberry**
**1 ½ cups sugar**
**1 6-ounce container of frozen orange juice concentrate**
**1 6-ounce container of frozen lemonade concentrate**
**8 cups cold water**
**1 quart ginger ale or lemon lime soda**

1. Mix together all ingredients except for the ginger ale or soda in a 4-quarter pitcher or large container.
2. Chill, overnight.
3. Add half of the mixture to a punch bowl.
4. Top with half of the ginger ale (½ quart).
5. Serve immediately.

### Tidbits from Jen's Kitchen

An ice ring jazzes up your punch presentation and is simple to make. Fill a bundt pan to within an inch of the top with a mixture of equal parts of your favorite fruit juice (pineapple is my favorite) and a flavored soda such as strawberry, raspberry or lemon lime. Add sliced strawberries or another fruit of your choice. Freeze for at least 8 hours or overnight. Unmold and transfer to your punch bowl before adding the punch.

**Megan's Recipe Secret:**

Use organic lemonade concentrate whenever possible to avoid high-fructose sugars.

**Megan's Recipe Secret:**

For fun, I used rainbow sherbet. It was groovy, baby!

# SHERBERT PUNCH

*serves 20*

Sherbet and ice cream punches were the "fad" when I was in high school in the 1980s. This was the punch that I requested for my high school graduation party. It is fluffy, fruity and just a little fancy. There are many variations of sherbet punch, almost as many as there are Jell-O salad recipes. This was my favorite version with lime sherbet. Raspberry sherbet comes in a close second.

1. Scoop frozen sherbet into a large punch bowl.
2. Add pineapple juice and ginger ale.
3. Stir until sherbet is partially melted.
4. Serve immediately.

**1 ½-gallon carton lime sherbet (or your favorite flavor)**
**1 46-ounce can pineapple juice**
**1 2-liter bottle ginger ale or lemon lime soda, or to taste**

**Tidbits from Jen's Kitchen**

Punch seems to have gone by the wayside these days and you don't see it at family celebrations like you did when I was growing up. For a modern twist, you can turn this fruity punch into a cocktail by swapping out half or all of the ginger ale for Prosecco.

# HOT COCOA MIX

*serves 32*

This recipe was a favorite of my friends and our cousins when we were young. We used to make it in an empty ice cream pail. Afterwards, you can freeze the mix right in the pail. It is then ready for your next bonfire or to warm you up on a cold night!

It is also a quick and easy homemade gift during the holidays. Simply make up a big batch and then package into canning jars. Add a ribbon tied around the lid along with the recipe and instructions to prepare. You now have a tasty little gift ready to share with your friends or family.

---

**1 16-ounce can instant chocolate milk mix**
**1 16-ounce jar powdered non-dairy coffee creamer**
**1 25.6-ounce package dry milk powder, enough to make 8 quarts**
**1 ½ cups powdered sugar**
**marshmallows, for garnish**

1. Mix all ingredients except marshmallows in a large bowl or an empty 5-quart ice cream pail or other freezer-safe container.
2. Store in the freezer until ready to use.
3. To Serve, boil water in a teapot. Add ½ cup mix plus 1 cup boiling water to make 1 cup of cocoa. Stir to combine. Don't forget to top with marshmallows before serving!

**Megan's Recipe Secret:**

Use a high quality chocolate powder to elevate your cocoa mix.

# Hearty Soups & Great Big Salads

Soups were served on the farmhouse table daily throughout the week. Mom and Dad loved their Campbell's soup, and still do.

I love to make soup throughout the year, perhaps it was because it was a lunchtime staple on our farmhouse table. In the winter, Mom would throw together a big batch of her vegetable beef soup featured in this collection. It was loaded with root vegetables and hearty enough to serve for dinner.

When it came to salads, there were generally two types – simple salads for weeknight dinners or potluck- friendly salad for gatherings and social events. On the farmhouse dinner table, we had a small salad most nights. It could be just a bit of iceberg with bottled dressing, sliced cucumbers or tomatoes when in season, or coleslaw. Nothing too fancy, just a simple side.

Potluck-friendly salads were a mainstay of family gatherings and social events - coleslaw, potato and pudding salads. These big batch salads graced most buffet tables, and there were endless variations!

This section includes some of my favorite soups and salads from our family's recipe collection along with a few of my own variations of the classics that graced our farmhouse table growing up. With this collection, we hope to share through pictures, stories and memories how hearty soups and great big salads were core to our childhood Minnesota dinner table.

*Rebecca, Jen, Randy (Rebecca's husband) and Mom about to enjoy some great big salads at the holidays.*

# MOM'S VEGETABLE BEEF SOUP
*serves 12*

My mom would make a big batch of this soup during the winter. It would fill the whole house with the smell of beef, vegetables and spices simmering on the stove. It is the definition of comfort food. Years later, this soup became the very first recipe I cooked professionally as a personal chef in Virginia Beach. My client hired me to prepare several large batches of soup for her team as she wanted to provide an easy hot option for a healthy in-the-office lunch. She selected this soup from my collection of options. This soup then landed my next assignment as her personal chef for her family. Simple, quality ingredients made with love can win over the hearts and tummies of many.

---

**Beef Broth:**
- 1 ½ pounds beef soup bones
- 1 teaspoon salt
- pepper, to taste
- ½ teaspoon garlic powder
- ½ teaspoon chili powder
- 4 tablespoons dried parsley
- 3 quarts water

**Soup:**
- ¼ cup pearl barley
- 1 cup chopped celery
- 1 cup chopped onions
- 1 cup ½-inch cubed baby carrots
- 1 cup ½-inch cubed new potatoes
- 1 cup ½-inch cubed rutabaga
- 4 cups stewed tomatoes

1. Combine all broth ingredients in a 6-quart soup pot. Bring to a boil; reduce heat and cover.
2. Boil gently on low heat for 3 hours.
3. Allow to cool. Refrigerate overnight.
4. Remove fat that has hardened on the top of the pot and discard. Reserving broth, meat and soup bones.
5. Pull remaining meat from soup bones.
6. Return meat to soup pot and discard bones. Add remaining soup ingredients and enough water to come within about 1-2-inches of the top of the soup pot.
7. Bring to a boil. Reduce heat and cover; boil gently for 2 hours, or until vegetables are tender.

**Tidbits from Jen's Kitchen**

I like to spice my recipes up a bit more than my parents do, so both the garlic & chili spices have been doubled from the original recipe. Feel free to adjust the seasonings to your individual taste.

**Megan's Recipe Secret:**

I didn't have beef soup bones on hand. Instead, I used beef stew meat and added beef bouillon.

**Megan's Recipe Secret:**

I'm partial to using fresh local tomatoes whenever possible. So for this recipe, I used roasted tomatoes from the garden that I froze from the previous summer. Tomato-y perfection!

# TOMATO SOUP

*serves* 4

Grilled cheese and tomato soup! Yum! One of my favorite farmhouse lunches. I may have mentioned this once before, but Mom and Dad really do love their Campbell's soup, and that includes tomato.

The lunchtime soup rotation was split pea with ham, bean and bacon, chicken noodle, cream of mushroom (yes, they actually used it to make soup and not just casseroles) as well as tomato. Sometimes, we might have chicken and rice. And, I considered chicken and stars a special treat, when Mom would buy it.

In my version of tomato soup, I have taken the classic canned Campbell's soup and jazzed it up. I have made this recipe for my parents before, and it received their approval. Mom even asked for the recipe!

Make yourself a gooey grilled cheese on some fresh baked bread and dunk your sandwich in the soup on a cold winter day! It will warm you from the inside out.

---

1. To a medium saucepan, add the tomatoes, soup and half and half. Simmer over medium-low to medium heat for 5-8 minutes until warmed through, stirring often. Do not boil or the soup will curdle.
2. Just before serving, stir in basil.
3. Serve immediately. Garnish with grated parmesan cheese and parsley.

**1 14 ½-ounce can of tomatoes, diced with basil, oregano and garlic**
**1 10 ½-ounce can of condensed tomato soup**
**1 ½ cups half and half (milk or whipping cream)**
**½ cup thinly sliced fresh basil leaves**
**grated parmesan cheese, for garnish**
**minced fresh parsley, for garnish**

SOUPS AND SALADS

# BEER CHEESE SOUP

*serves 6*

The Grainery restaurant in Fargo, North Dakota was a much-loved place for lunch when we "girls" (Mom, my sister, Rebecca and I) ventured out for our semi-annually shopping trip to the West Acres mall. I loved the beer cheese soup at the Grainery; it was a requirement for a successful shopping trip. It was sinfully rich and cheesy goodness in a bowl topped with salty and crunchy movie theater-style popcorn. This soup was so popular locally that the restaurant supplied it to the local groceries for sale in their deli departments!

The Grainery was located in West Acres, our closest indoor shopping mall. It opened in Fargo, North Dakota, in 1972. Before that the next closest indoor shopping malls were in Minneapolis, Minnesota, which was over a 3-hour drive away. Cutting the travel time in half changed shopping in our farming community dramatically. West Acres also housed the first Dayton's department store outside of Minnesota when it opened in 1973. The hour and half drive to Fargo to shop indoors, especially during the heart of the cold winter, was an adventure that my sister and I looked forward to each time.

We would plan our shopping trips around back to school shopping and then for President's Day, as that was when the stores had the best deals. The West Acres mall has survived the test of time, celebrating nearly 40 years of indoor shopping in 2020. However, the Grainery, sadly, no longer exists. The owner of the Grainery sold the restaurant in 2001. It was closed and reopened as a bar and grill. My memories of the Grainery live on through this recipe from my archives, which has been adapted from a version I found years back that claimed to be the "original" from the Grainery.

---

½ cup flour
½ cup butter or margarine
4 cups chicken broth
1 16-ounce jar of Cheez Whiz pasteurized process cheese spread
1 ½ cups sour cream
6 ounces beer, or more to taste
1 tablespoon Worcestershire sauce
pinch or two turmeric
¼ cup chives, minced
popcorn (optional)

1. Melt butter and flour. Cook over low heat for about 5 minutes.
2. Gradually add broth and cream stirring constantly to keep the mixture smooth. Cook until thickened.
3. Once the soup has thickened, add cheese stirring until melted and well blended.
4. Add beer, Worcestershire sauce and a pinch or two of turmeric. Simmer for about 15 minutes.
5. Top with popcorn and chives.

### Tidbits from Jen's Kitchen

I prefer to use turmeric to enhance the yellow color instead of food coloring, as included in the original recipe. Use a light beer for the classic flavor of the original soup or experiment with a micro-brew like a porter or an IPA to create a modern twist on this Midwestern classic soup.

SOUPS AND SALADS

**Homemade "Cheez Whiz"**

No Cheez Whiz? No problem! You make your own by simply adding the following ingredients to your chicken broth when it calls to add the Cheez Whiz recipe above.

2 teaspoons cornstarch
½ teaspoon salt
½ teaspoon garlic powder
½ teaspoon onion powder
2 teaspoons mustard powder
1 cup half and half
4 ounces of cream cheese, cut into cubes
2 cups shredded American cheese (from a block)

**Megan's Recipe Secret:**

As a former vegetarian, chili was the best when I needed to clean out the vegetables in my fridge or freezer. I like to toss vegetables, beans, tomatoes, and spices in a soup pot – and voila, it's chili! Even while making this recipe, I snuck in extra ingredients – like summer squash, corn, black beans, and kidney beans. There are infinite possible varieties to a chili recipe!

# MOM'S CHILI

*serves 6*

Chili and cornbread were a hearty farmhouse meal during the winter months. Mom would serve her chili with fresh baked cornbread slathered with butter or grilled cheese sandwiches.

Many of the recipes in my collection from back in the day called for hamburger instead of ground beef. It is less common today to see hamburger offered at the grocery store or at the meat market. My parents purchased our beef from local farms, and it was processed by the butcher in town, so our ground beef was hamburger. Hamburger is a cut of meat which can contain any of the primal beef cuts while ground beef is generally a single cut such as ground round or ground sirloin. Hamburger cannot contain any more than 30% total fat, but it can have fat added directly to the mix. Ground beef cannot have added fat. If you see a recipe that calls for hamburger, ground beef is a perfectly acceptable substitute.

---

1. In a large soup pot, sauté onion (along with the celery and peppers if you are using them) in a bit of butter. Add in ground beef and brown.
2. Combine remaining ingredients and simmer, the longer the better.
3. Serve in individual bowls topped with cheddar cheese, diced onions and sour cream.

**1 large onion, diced**
**diced celery (optional)**
**green pepper (optional)**
**butter**
**1 pound hamburger (ground beef)**
**1 teaspoon salt**
**1 ¼ teaspoons chili powder**
**1 8-ounce can tomato sauce**
**1 tablespoon white vinegar**
**2 tablespoons brown sugar**
**cheddar cheese, diced onions and sour cream, for topping**

**Tidbits from Jen's Kitchen**

I like a little bit more tomato in my chili, so I double the amount of tomato sauce from that listed below. For a chunkier variation you can opt to use diced tomatoes. This is a fairly mild chili so feel free to up the chili powder to your own liking.

SOUPS AND SALADS

# POTATO SOUP

*serves 6*

We always planted many hills of potatoes in our garden each year. To this day, Dad plants potatoes each year in his garden on the farm. Some years, when my Uncle Reynold Ellingson was still alive, we would receive potatoes by the bushel when he had a bumper crop. One year, as my dad recalls, Uncle Reynold had over 3,000 pounds of potatoes harvested from his family farm located near ours! Dad would store our potato stash in the cold, dark storage room in our basement. We would head into the winter months loaded down with potatoes.

Potatoes graced the dinner table frequently in the form of boiled potatoes on the stove top, tinfoil-wrapped baked potatoes or even potato "patties" made from leftover potatoes. Mashed potatoes were reserved for special occasions.

Potato soup was a great way to use up potatoes as they aged over the winter months. This comforting soup is good for the soul on a cold winter day. It is a soup I still make today, especially after Easter when there is leftover ham readily available.

---

5 large potatoes, washed, peeled and diced
½ cup diced carrots
6 slices of uncooked bacon
4 stalks celery, chopped
2 medium onions, chopped
1 ½ teaspoons salt
¼ teaspoon white peppers
2 cups milk
2 cups light cream or evaporated milk
1 cup diced cooked smoked ham
1 cup cheddar cheese
minced chives or parsley
dash paprika

1. Clean, peel, then dice potatoes. Cook with carrots in boiling water until tender. Drain.
2. Sauté bacon until crisp tender in a skillet. Remove bacon, place on a paper towel-lined plate and then crumble when cool.
3. Drain grease from the skillet, reserving 2 tablespoons of bacon fat.
4. Sauté onion and celery in bacon fat.
5. Combine all ingredients (except the cheese, ham, paprika and chives) in a soup pot. Simmer for 30 minutes.
6. Add in ham. Simmer for 5 minutes more, until the ham is warmed through.
7. Serve in individual bowls and garnish with chives, cheddar cheese, and a pinch or two of paprika.

SOUPS AND SALADS

**Megan's Recipe Secret:**

I accidentally added the cheese to the soup pot before serving, and I do not regret it one bit.

# BROCCOLI SUPREME SALAD
*serves a bunch*

This classic Midwestern salad appeared at many potluck and family celebrations as it was hearty enough to be made ahead of time. It is a great make-ahead salad because it tastes better the longer it marinates.

---

1. In a small bowl, whisk all dressing ingredients together.
2. In a large mixing bowl, add all the salad ingredients and drizzle with dressing. Toss salad to coat all the ingredients.
3. Marinate in the refrigerator for at least 2 hours.

**Dressing:**
1 cup mayonnaise
½ cup sugar
½ teaspoon garlic powder
salt, to taste
pepper, to taste
1 tablespoon white or apple cider vinegar
1 teaspoon lemon juice

**Salad:**
4 cups broccoli, cut up into bite size pieces
4 heads cauliflower, cut up into bite sized pieces
¾ cup raisins, regular or golden
1 small red onion, in thin slices or finely diced
4 green onions, chopped
½ pound bacon, cooked and crumbled
¼ cup slivered almonds or sunflower seeds
⅓ - ½ cup Cheddar cheese, shredded (optional)

---

**Tidbits from Jen's Kitchen**

If you are not a fan of cauliflower, you can make the salad with only broccoli. I use champagne or white balsamic vinegar because they are not as bold or as harsh as white or apple cider. I don't remember having anything other than plain white or apple cider in the farm pantry. I discovered the wide variety of options for vinegar much later in life.

Swap out the broccoli and cauliflower florets for store-bought broccoli and carrot slaw for a quick and modern twist on this salad.

For a healthier variation, you can simply use Greek yogurt instead of mayonnaise. You can also leave the sugar out completely or replace it with ¼ cup of honey.

SOUPS AND SALADS

# CABBAGE SALAD

*serves 12*

Cabbage salad was often made with a vinegar dressing as it would keep well for days. This is the recipe that Mom would take to potlucks or family events because you could make it in advance. It was also a great option for a buffet where it might sit out without refrigeration for a bit.

---

4 cups cabbage, coarsely chopped cabbage
1 large red or green pepper, chopped
1 small bunch carrots, grated or shredded
1 small onion, diced
sliced radishes or chopped celery (optional)
½ cup vegetable oil
½ cup vinegar
½ cup sugar
salt, to taste
pepper, to taste

1. In a large mixing bowl, add vegetables and drizzle with oil.
2. In a small saucepan, heat vinegar and sugar over medium-low heat until sugar dissolves completely. Cool.
3. Pour vinegar mix over vegetables. Toss to coat.
4. Season with salt and pepper.
5. Refrigerate 1-2 hours before serving, or overnight.

**Megan's Recipe Secret:**

In the winter, I frequently make variations of this cabbage salad. Cabbage, carrots, and onions are often found in my winter CSA farm share. Coleslaw is a versatile side that you can jazz up with lime juice and cilantro for tacos or top with a poppy seed dressing for another wonderful variation.

# COLESLAW DRESSING

*serves 12*

Coleslaw remains a side dish that my parents both still like to make and serve at least weekly, if not more often.

Mom's recipe for the dressing is made with Miracle Whip. Until moving south, I thought that Miracle Whip salad dressing and mayonnaise were the same thing, after all you found them in the same aisle right next to each other. To be clear, they are not the same.

During the Depression, Miracle Whip was cheaper than mayonnaise. Many families in the north would become Miracle Whip lovers as a result. Miracle Whip is considered a salad dressing as its oil content is not high enough to meet the definition of mayonnaise, or at least 65%. Miracle Whip also contains sugar, which sets it apart from mayonnaise, which traditionally does not contain added sugar.

Truth be told, you can use either one in this dressing. It is really up to you! It might even be a fun experiment and make it both ways. Then, do a taste test to find out if you are more of a northerner or a southerner when it comes to coleslaw.

---

1. Combine all ingredients together and whisk to blend.
2. Season with garlic powder, salt and pepper, to taste.
3. Refrigerate until ready to use.

**1 cup regular Miracle Whip salad dressing**
**½ cup chopped or grated onions, or more to taste**
**1 tablespoon seasoned rice vinegar, or more to taste**
**1 tablespoon sugar, or less to taste**
**6 tablespoons milk**
**1 tablespoon yellow mustard**
**garlic powder, salt and pepper, to taste**
**shredded carrots, optional**
**green onion, minced, optional**

*Tidbits from Jen's Kitchen*

The recipe makes enough dressing to coat 6 to 8 cups of shredded cabbage. Coleslaw is best if combined in the morning for an evening meal. You can add in shredded carrots and minced green onion, if desired, as my mom often did. Mom's recipe twist, handwritten on the card, suggested using this dressing for a vegetable salad with cauliflower and other chopped vegetables.

SOUPS AND SALADS

# CREAMY CUCUMBER SALAD
*serves 4*

We always had a huge garden on the farm, or at least it seemed that way to my sister, Rebecca, and I growing up. Gardening was not my preferred chore. I would rather iron, and that says a lot.

Despite many summers hoeing, weeding and watering the garden I did not develop a green thumb. That gift skipped a generation to my daughter, Megan. Instead, I rely on my local produce and farmer's markets to procure the closest I can find to fresh produce like we had from our garden each summer.

The garden on our farm had many hills of cucumbers to ensure we had enough to can pickles. Those cucumbers that were too large to be used for canning were set aside and often turned into this simple salad. Nowadays I opt for the English cucumbers, but you can use any variety of cucumber in this salad. If your cucumbers have very large seeds, cut the cucumber in half lengthwise and then scrape the seeds out of both halves of the cucumber. Then cut the cucumber into cute little half-moons.

---

½ cup sour cream or plain yogurt
1 tablespoon vinegar or lemon juice
1 teaspoon sugar
¼ teaspoon dried dill
pepper, to taste
1 teaspoon salt
1 large cucumber or enough for 3 cups, halved and cut into thin slices
1 small sweet onion, thinly sliced

1. Stir together sour cream, vinegar, sugar and dill in a medium bowl. Add cucumber and onion. Toss to combine. Season with salt and pepper.
2. Chill before serving.

**Tidbits from Jen's Kitchen**

If you want to prevent your cucumber salad from getting too watery in the refrigerator, you can salt them after you slice them and let them sit for 20 minutes in a colander to drain away some of the excess moisture.

SOUPS AND SALADS

**Megan's Recipe Secret:**

I recommend making this salad in the summer when produce is in season. The veggies are much more crisp and flavorful. You can adapt this as a salad in a jar for work, just assemble in opposite order.

# SEVEN LAYER SALAD

*serves 12*

This recipe is another Midwestern classic, frequently served at potlucks and picnics. The history of the seven layer salad dates back to the 1950s. Iceberg was the lettuce of choice. Believe it or not, it does not get soggy. The vegetable layers for a protective barrier between the iceberg lettuce and the dressing. Be sure to seed your tomatoes before adding them to the salad for extra protection of your iceberg lettuce.

This salad is also a great one to "play" with, interchanging the ingredient layers to create a whole profile. Try it "Italian-style". Swap the ham for pepperoni. Use crushed croutons and parmesan cheese instead of cheddar. Then sprinkle top with a bit of smoked paprika. You can also add in a couple of tablespoons of grated Parmesan to your dressing too. Want to dress it up a bit for a make-ahead dinner party salad? Make and service in individual glass bowls.

---

1. Place lettuce on the bottom of a glass serving bowl or a 9x13-inch glass cake pan, or a fancy glass bowl if you have one. Add vegetables on top in layers, as listed.
2. Mix sour cream, mayonnaise, sugar and seasoning. Spread over the top.
3. Sprinkle cheese over the top and then ham and bacon.
4. Refrigerate for at least 8 hours before serving.

1 head iceberg lettuce, chopped
1 10-ounce package frozen green peas
1 large carrot, grated
1 cup celery, diced
4 hard boiled eggs, chopped or shredded
½ cup green bell peppers, diced
1 red onion, finely diced or 1 bunch green onions, minced
2-3 roma tomatoes, diced
1 cup sour cream (or Greek yogurt)
1 cup mayonnaise
1 teaspoon seasoned salt
¼ teaspoon garlic powder
2 tablespoons sugar
½ pound sharp cheddar cheese, grated
1 package bacon, cooked and crumbled
1 cup finely cut strips of ham

**Tidbits from Jen's Kitchen**

I like to add a bit more punch to the dressing. A splash or two of white balsamic vinegar plus a ½ teaspoon or more of Old Bay, blackening seasoning or your favorite steak or poultry blend, matching the flavor profile with the main course that the salad will be paired with. You can also give this classic a modern-day twist by exchanging the iceberg for chopped romaine, kale or a combination of both.

SOUPS AND SALADS

# AUNT EUNICE'S SHRIMP SALAD

*serves 12*

Potlucks were an annual summertime event for our family. We would gather at the lake for the fourth of July at one location or another. As you have come to know by now with my dad's large extended family, gatherings really only had one option for feeding the whole bunch – a potluck. Summertime pasta salads were a make-ahead, go-to dish that was crowd friendly.

This shrimp pasta salad has a Crab Louie-like dressing that the pasta readily absorbs. If you like your pasta salad a bit more on the creamy and saucy side, make extra dressing, reserving some to add just before serving.

If you are like me, you may not be a huge fan of raw green bell pepper. Skip that if you'd like or add in a red or orange bell pepper instead. I like to increase the amount of bell pepper and cucumber when I make this salad. The chunkier the better!

---

**Dressing:**
1 cup Miracle Whip salad dressing (or mayonnaise)
½ cup French salad dressing
¼ teaspoon dry mustard

**Salad:**
½ cup diced celery
1 tablespoon diced onions
1 tablespoon diced green peppers

1 tablespoon diced cucumber
2 6-ounce bags of frozen peeled and deveined salad shrimp
1 7-ounce package shell pasta, cooked according to package directions and cooled

1. Thaw shrimp. Rinse with cold water. Drain with a colander.
2. In a small bowl or an empty mason jar, add Miracle Whip, French salad dressing and whisk to combine.
3. In a large bowl, toss together the celery, onions, green pepper, cucumber and shrimp with cooked shell pasta.
4. Drizzle dressing over the top of the salad and stir to coat salad ingredients.
5. Refrigerate for 6 hours or overnight.

**Tidbits from Jen's Kitchen**

Looking for an updated version of this salad? Skip the pasta and serve in half of a ripe, hollowed-out tomato or serve it deconstructed over a wedge of iceberg lettuce with medium-sized shrimp instead of the little guys.

SOUPS AND SALADS

**Megan's Recipe Secret:**

I LOVED this dressing. It goes wonderfully with homemade sauerkraut on a hot Rachel (aka Reuben with Turkey) sandwich.

# THOUSAND ISLAND DRESSING

*serves 8*

Salad dressings on our farmhouse table were either Ranch (made from a package of dry mix, you know the one) or a bottled dressing - French or Thousand Island. Weeknight dinners most often included a simple side salad of iceberg lettuce, maybe a few croutons and was tossed in one of these dressings.

Nowadays, I love to make my own dressing. This recipe is my take on Thousand Island that I grew up with but with a kick. If you prefer a milder version, cut back on the paprika and the chili powder.

---

1. In a medium bowl, combine all ingredients, except spices. For a less chunky version, use a mini food processor or an immersion blender and process until smooth.
2. Add spices (paprika, chili powder, seasoning salt and pepper) slowly, tasting along the way to get the flavor profile that works for you.
3. Chill before serving to allow flavors to blend.

1 clove garlic, minced or grated
1 cup mayonnaise
2 tablespoons shallots, minced
3-4 tablespoons pickle relish
2 tablespoons ketchup
1-2 tablespoons cilantro
1 teaspoon smoked Spanish paprika (mild)
1 tablespoon chili powder, or to taste
1 teaspoon seasoning salt
½ teaspoon pepper
water, as needed

SOUPS AND SALADS

# BANANA CREAM SALAD

*serves 16*

Is this recipe a salad or dessert? Either way, it is another classic that my mom would make for potlucks and family get-togethers. In my mind, this is dessert. I would go back and get it for "seconds" at a potluck because I did not want this sweet treat of a salad to get mixed up with my savory first plate selections.

Dessert salads are a Minnesota "thing." From what I understand, the history of the dessert salad flows from our Scandinavian roots. Dessert salads were historically (and still) served in big bowls and reserved for large gatherings and special occasions. These salads did not grace the farmhouse table at a regular weeknight meal.

Whether you decide to serve this as a salad or a dessert, I hope you enjoy this tasty family version of a Scandinavian dessert salad.

---

**2 5.1-ounce packages of banana cream pudding (or 3 3.4-ounce packages)**
**2 cups milk**
**1 8-ounce container of frozen whipped topping**
**1 ½ cups small marshmallows**
**1 can sweetened condensed milk**
**6 bananas, sliced**
**½-1 cup walnuts, chopped (optional)**

1. In a Dutch oven, bring pudding to a bubbling boil with milk. Keep boiling for a fair amount of time until it is good and thick. Cool.
2. Add sweetened condensed milk, marshmallows and whipped topping and stir to combine. Refrigerate.
3. Add in sliced bananas and walnuts (if using) just before serving. Stir to combine.

SOUPS AND SALADS

# CHERRY COKE SALAD

*serves 8-12*

Jell-O or congealed salads were another Midwestern classic from my childhood. Cherry Coke salad would make its annual appearance on our holiday dinner table at the farm. It's festive and gets a nice tang from the Coca Cola, or Coke as we called it. It is quite beautiful if you can find a glass or crystal bowl to prepare and serve this salad.

It is a great example of a congealed salad which were popular during my childhood and in Minnesota. These salads have their roots in Europe but were transformed in America during the early 1900s. James Beard observed, in the 1972 edition of James Beard's American Cookery that it was the 1905 victory of the Perfection Salad at the World's Fair that "unleashed a demand for congealed salads that has grown alarmingly, particularly in the suburbs." The Perfection Salad took third place, as I understand it, and was a congealed concoction using Knox gelatin. Then during the war years, congealed salads became a way to affordably entertain despite rations and shortages.

While you can find Jell-O salads in most parts of the country, what sets Minnesota apart is our Scandinavian heritage that turns it into a dessert salad. Scandinavians brought Rømmegrøt to America, a thick and creamy rice pudding-type dish which has characteristics similar to the dessert salads developed later in Minnesota.

---

1. In a medium size bowl, combine boiling water and Jell-O and stir until sugar is dissolved. Add remaining ingredients. Stir to combine.
2. Chill to set.
3. Top with whipped topping once the Jell-O has set.

**1 6-ounce (double size) package cherry Jell-O**
**1 cup boiling water**
**1 21-ounce can of cherry pie filling**
**1 ½ cups Coca Cola ("Coke")**
**1 8-ounce container whipped topping**

SOUPS AND SALADS

*At Our Farmhouse Table*

*Daddy's little helpers.*

   This section is a collection of some of the entrees and sides that appeared on our table for breakfast, lunch or dinner whether it was a weeknight meal, a Sunday supper or special occasion dish. There are also a few recipes from our extended family that bring back fond memories from my childhood years, like Aunt Carolyn's rolls. I still remember sitting in her Breckenridge kitchen watching her make bread and rolls when I was stormed in for a day or two. Nothing is better than freshly baked bread or rolls with a little butter.

# AUNT CAROLYN'S ROLLS
*serves 16*

Growing up, Aunt Carolyn's bread and buns were hard to beat. Dad has always admired her bread baking skills. He would try to find out her secrets whenever he could. I am not sure anyone has really figured out her secrets completely, but this recipe that my mom shared with me for her bread is a great starting point to experiment with baking bread at home.

Of the two of us, my sister Rebecca became the bread baker, keeping the family tradition alive. She has become quite accomplished at it. Now Megan has started to bake bread too. I am glad to see this family tradition continue.

---

- 4 ¼-ounce packages yeast
- 1 cup powdered milk
- 5 cups of warm water, divided
- 1 cup sugar
- 2 tablespoons salt
- 3-4 large eggs
- 12-14 cups flour, divided
- 1 cup melted margarine

1. In a small bowl, add 1 cup of warm water to the yeast. Stir to combine.
2. In a large mixing bowl, combine yeast, powdered milk, remaining 4 cups of water, sugar, salt, eggs along with 8 cups of flour. Beat hard with an electric hand mixer. Stir in remaining flour by hand, adding a cup at a time.
3. Set aside for 20 minutes; knead. Let rise 2 more times.
4. Cut into buns or rolls. Let rise. While the buns or rolls rise the last time, preheat oven 350°F for buns or 325°F for finger rolls.
5. Bake for 12-15 minutes for buns. Bake for 10 minutes for finger rolls.

**Megan's Recipe Secret:**

I previously mis-judged how much these would rise in the oven. As a result, they were enormous buns. We enjoyed the extra-large buns for sandwiches (see Sloppy Joes recipe, Page 101). Expect the buns to double in size during the final proof.

# PAN-FRIED WALLEYE

*serves 4*

    Growing up in the land of ten thousand lakes meant that fishing was (and is) a common pastime. Fishing is a year-round sport for those brave enough to sit on the ice and fish during the winter.
    My best fish tale is from when I was quite young and went fishing with my dad and my cousin, Michael Ellingson, for the day. Michael would bait my line and also showed me how to cast. It was a fairly weedy lake so when my line was bent over and taught, Michael proclaimed I had a "bad case of the bottoms." He grabbed my line and proceeded to reel in a large northern pike. I don't remember how many pounds it was to be exact, but it was likely at least six or seven pounds. It was a nice catch, to say the least. I proceed to catch several more walleyes, most large enough to keep. I was the only one to catch "keepers" that day. I was told it must have been beginner's luck. I don't know if it was luck or just a light hand on the rod as I really wasn't paying much attention most of the time. I was just happy to be on the water!
    Walleye and northern pike are both delicious white fish found in lakes of Minnesota. They are an easy-to-prepare, mild and flaky white fish. My dad would pan fry our fresh catch with a saltine cracker crust. The key to getting the batter to stick is to pat the filets dry and then coat them lightly in flour before you coat them with eggs and then cracker crumbs.

---

1. Check the walleye filets to ensure all bones have been removed.
2. Place crackers in a resealable plastic bag. Roll with a rolling pin until they are finely crushed and have the consistency of breadcrumbs.
3. Place the beaten eggs in a pie plate or baking dish. Combine the flour, garlic powder, paprika, salt, and pepper in another pie plate or baking dish. Pour the cracker crumbs into a third pie plate or baking dish.
4. Coat the filets into the flour mixture. Shake off excess. Then transfer and coat both sides of the fish with the egg mixture. Finally, transfer to the cracker crumbs to coat. Set coated filets aside on a plate.
5. In a large cast-iron skillet over medium-high, heat 2-4 tablespoons of butter (enough to coat the bottom of the skillet generously). Carefully place 2 filets into the hot skillet. The filets should sizzle when placed in the skillet.
6. Cook until browned, about 2-3 minutes per side. Use a non-stick spatula or fish turner to turn the filets. The filets should release easily, if done. Transfer to a paper towel-lined plate.
7. Repeat with remaining filets, adding more butter, as needed.

**4 6-ounce walleye filets or other white fish**
**2 large eggs, beaten**
**a splash of milk**
**½ cup flour**
**½ teaspoon garlic powder**
**pinch or two paprika**
**pinch or two salt**
**¼ teaspoon white pepper**
**2 cups crushed saltine crackers**
**2-4 tablespoons butter (or more as needed to fry fish)**

OUR FARMHOUSE TABLE

# BROILED SALMON WITH ORANGE MISO GLAZE

*serves 6*

My sister Rebecca is seven years older than I. She met her husband, Randy Bissinger, while they were both attending the University of North Dakota (UND). Randy graduated from UND with his medical degree and accepted a residency in Seattle, Washington. Together they moved out west to begin their life adventures together. I was still in high school when they moved and extremely curious, ready to visit and explore!

Moving to the west coast, first in Seattle, Washington then to Corvallis and finally Salem, Oregon, my sister had access to seafood and fish that we didn't have available in rural Minnesota during the 1970s and into the 1980s. I remember visiting them in Seattle with my parents when I was a senior in high school. We went to the famous Pike's Place Fish Market. We purchased fresh crab for what I considered an at-home feast like nothing I had experienced before. I was in heaven, especially when Randy cracked and picked the crab legs for me!

My sister's West Coast salmon recipes are some of the best I have ever had. This salmon recipe is one of the first recipes that she gave me after moving Wasinghton state. It came with a few of her other favorite recipes in a pretty recipe box that matched my dishes. This is the recipe box that I still use to hold my family collection.

Together, she and I have exchanged many recipes over the years. We have lots of fun discussing recipes and techniques. It is a well-kept secret that I think she is a better cook than I am. Please don't tell her!

---

⅓ cup yellow miso (fermented soybean paste)
2 tablespoons orange juice
1 tablespoon mirin (sweet Japanese rice wine)
2 teaspoons soy sauce
1 teaspoon dark brown sugar
1 teaspoon grated orange peel
6 salmon filets or steelhead trout
finely chopped green onions

1. Whisk the first 6 ingredients together in a small bowl.
2. Preheat broiler to 500°F. Line a baking sheet with foil.
3. Place salmon on the baking sheet, skin side down. Spread miso glaze over salmon.
4. Broil salmon until it starts to blister and brown, about 7 minutes. Remove from the oven and cover salmon loosely with foil. Broil until cooked through, another 7 minutes.
5. Transfer to a plate and top with onions.

# CHICKEN AND TINY BISCUITS

*serves 12*

When I think of comfort food and my childhood, this is one dish that comes to mind. Essentially it is a chicken stew topped with biscuits baked until steamy and hot in the oven. Mom would make this dish in the cold winter months, and it was good food for your soul. If you need a time saver, you can purchase a deli chicken for this recipe and simply add in chicken stock or broth.

---

1. In a large pot or Dutch oven, boil chicken for about 1 hour on medium-high heat (about 350°F).
2. Drain chicken, reserving any drippings. Cool. Refrigerate the drippings to make it easier to skim the fat off while you take the chicken off the bone.
3. Preheat oven to 400°F.
4. Melt butter in a heavy saucepan. Add flour and blend until smooth. Gradually add chicken broth and milk. Add salt and pepper, to taste.
5. Arrange chicken in the bottom a 9x13-inch pan or a lasagna pan. (You may have enough for another small square 9x9-inch pan.) Pour sauce over chicken. Arrange tiny biscuits on top of the hot chicken mixture.
6. Bake for 25-30 minutes or until biscuits are done.
7. Garnish with parsley.

3 ½ cups chicken
6 cups chicken broth (including reserved from chicken)
1 cup flour
1 ½ cups milk
salt
pepper
9 tablespoons butter

**Tiny Biscuits:**
2 cups sifted flour
¼ teaspoon salt
2 ½ teaspoons baking powder
¼ teaspoon baking soda
6 tablespoons shortening
3/4 cup buttermilk
parsley, for garnish

Tiny Biscuits - yields 28

1. Sift flour and dry ingredients together. Cut in shortening until mixture resembles coarse crumbs. Add milk all at once and mix with a fork, just until dough follows the fork around the bowl.
2. Turn onto a floured surface; need gently for 30 seconds. Roll out lightly to ½-inch thick. Cut into 28 biscuits with a biscuit cutter.

OUR FARMHOUSE TABLE

# IMPERIAL CHICKEN

*serves 4*

This recipe is a great Sunday supper for a rainy or cold day. You can't go wrong with a roast chicken.

Mom and Dad would purchase our chickens from one of the neighboring farmers. Once I went to college, I discovered that "country" chickens were much larger than a "city" chicken, or a store-bought chicken.

Shopping for meat at the grocery store was one of my great disappointments when I first went away to college. I now realize how blessed I was to have been raised on a farm with some of the best meats and poultry around. I am thankful that local butcher shops and community farms are springing back up to help bring us closer to the quality we had growing up in Minnesota farm country.

---

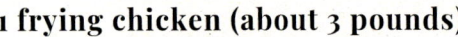

**1 frying chicken (about 3 pounds)**
**⅓ cup butter, melted**
**1 cup fine dry breadcrumbs**
**¼ cup parmesan cheese**
**2 tablespoons parsley**
**1 clove garlic or generous pinch of garlic powder**
**1 teaspoon salt**
**¼ teaspoon pepper**

1. Preheat oven to 375°F.
2. Cut the chicken into pieces. Pat dry with paper towels.
3. Coat each piece of chicken with butter.
4. Combine breadcrumbs, parmesan cheese, parsley, garlic, salt and pepper together in a shallow bowl or pie plate. Roll chicken in crumbs thoroughly to coat.
5. Place on a greased sheet pan. Drip any remaining butter over the top.
6. Bake uncovered at 375°F for 45 minutes to 1 hour.
7. A large chicken or multiple chickens requires a longer baking time. Bake for 45 minutes at 375 °F to start. Then reduce the heat to 300-325°F and continue cooking for up to another 45 minutes.

**Tidbits from Jen's Kitchen**

I am a huge fan of a digital meat thermometer. After 45 minutes in the oven, check the temperature of the chicken and see if it is nearing 165°F in the thickest parts. Check every 15 minutes until done. On average, estimate 1 hour for an average sized "city" chicken.

**Megan's Recipe Secret:**

I love to smother meatloaf with gravy instead of ketchup or tomato sauce.

# LOADED VEGETABLE MEATLOAF
*serves 4*

Meatloaf is a classic Midwest comfort food, but it can often be a little bland. As you can see from the recipes included in this collection, we liked to add lots of vegetables to our dishes. Onion, celery and green peppers were added to just about everything! This recipe is no exception. The vegetables take this dish from bland to a main course entrée rich in flavor. Feel free to add or adjust the vegetables included to your own taste.

Mom would top her meatloaf with a tomato sauce. I am not a fan of tomato sauce topped meatloaf. I am not a fan of meatloaf topped tomato gravy nor really any sauce for that matter. I consider myself more of a meatloaf "purist" as a good meatloaf doesn't need to be drenched in sauce and can hold its own. As a self-proclaimed purist, I didn't capture the recipe for mom's tomato gravy in my recipe archives. My memory has it loosely recorded as mostly ketchup with perhaps a bit of mustard and a couple tablespoons of brown sugar.

---

1. Preheat oven to 350°F.
2. In a large bowl combine egg, breadcrumbs, liquid, vegetables and seasonings. Add ground beef. Mix until combined. Do no over mix.
3. Pat into a 7x3x2-inch loaf pan or shape into a circle with a 6-inch diameter on a sheet pan. Then form a 2-inch diameter hole in the middle.
4. Bake for 45-50 minutes for a loaf or 25-30 minutes for a ring.

1 large egg, beaten
¾ cup soft breadcrumbs (1 slice) or
¼ cup dried breadcrumbs
¼ cup milk or beer
¼ cup finely chopped onions or 1 tablespoon dried minced onion
¼ cup finely chopped celery
¼ cup finely chopped green peppers
¼ cup shredded carrots (optional)
1 8-ounce package mushrooms (optional)
2 tablespoons snipped parsley
½ teaspoon dried sage
½ teaspoon basil or oregano
½ teaspoon thyme
½ teaspoon salt
¼ teaspoon pepper
1 pound ground beef

**Tidbits from Jen's Kitchen**

I have grown to appreciate the taste of thyme more than I did when I was younger. You may want to try cutting it back from the ½ teaspoon in the original recipe as it is still a bit too much for me. I substitute herbs de Provence instead of 100% thyme.

# CLASSIC BEEF POT ROAST

*serves 6-8*

Cold winter nights on the farm called for hearty food. Beef roast in the oven was one of those comforting dishes that mom would prepare for our family. Some nights she would braise the beef with potatoes and carrots like the version below. Other times it was just a simple and humble roast on a bed of onions.

---

**3 lbs boneless beef chuck pot roast**
**2 tsp salt, divided**
**½ tsp fresh ground black pepper**
**½ tsp garlic powder**
**2 tbsp vegetable oil**
**1 large onion, sliced into half-moons,**
**2 cups beef broth**
**½ tsp herbs de Provence**
**2 bay leaves**
**1 tbsp tomato paste**
**4 tsp Worcestershire sauce**
**6 medium carrots, peeled and cut into 1 ½-inch pieces**
**4 medium white russet potatoes, peeled and cut into 1 ½-inch pieces**
**4 tbsp flour**
**1 cup milk**

1. Arrange a rack in the middle of the oven and preheat to 325°F.
2. Season the roast with 1 ½ teaspoons of salt, pepper and garlic powder.
3. Heat the oil in a Dutch oven over medium-high heat until hot and it starts to simmer. Add the roast and brown on all sides. Remove roast from the Dutch oven and set aside.
4. Reduce the heat to medium and add the onions to the Dutch oven and remaining ½ teaspoon salt. Sauté until onions soften and begin to brown around the edges.
5. Add in a ½ cup of beef stock to deglaze the pan. Stir in the beef broth, herbs de Provence, bay leaves, tomato paste, and Worcestershire sauce. Return the meat to the pan along with any juices.
6. Bring to a simmer, then cover and place in the oven. Braise for 1 ½ hours. The meat should appear tender but will not be falling apart yet.
7. Uncover and add the carrots and potatoes into the Dutch oven around the roast. Cover and return to the oven. Braise until the roast pulls apart easily and the vegetables are tender but not mushy, about 1 ½ hours more.
8. Remove meat and vegetables from the pan and place on a serving platter. Cover with tin foil while you make the pan gravy.
9. Add 4 tablespoons of flour to 1 cup of milk and whisk to combine. Stir slowly into Dutch oven and whisk until combined. Simmer gravy on medium to medium-high heat until gravy thickens, whisking continually.
10. Serve gravy alongside beef and vegetables.

**What is a hotdish? Let's break it down. It should have:**

- Protein: ground beef, chicken, tuna.
- Vegetables: canned or frozen, such as corn, peas and carrots, green beans, broccoli.
- Starch: wild or regular rice, pasta, mashed potatoes, tater tots.
- Binder: canned cream soup such as mushroom, celery, chicken or cheddar.
- Toppings: fried onions, chow mein noodles, nuts, crushed corn flakes or potato chips.

# WILD RICE HOTDISH

*serves 8*

Hot dish and wild rice both represent our Minnesota roots. I thought everyone knew what a hotdish was. Then I moved to Iowa to attend college at the University of Iowa. It was then discovered that no, it was truly a Minnesota "thing."

The hotdish, let me suggest, is the unofficial cuisine of the state of Minnesota. The documentary "Minnesota Hotdish: A Love Story" suggests that the Great Depression established hotdish as a Minnesota food staple. A hotdish was, and still is, an effective, affordable way of feeding entire families, with canned food and readily available meats.

The first recorded hot dish recipe was in a Lutheran cookbook from Mankato, Minnesota published in the 1930s. It was in 1934 when the Campbell Soup Company introduced its line of creamed soups. Cream of mushroom soup has since been termed the Lutheran hotdish "binder".

Wild rice has been the state grain of Minnesota since 1977. This grain grows naturally in crystal clear, cool waters of northern Minnesota. The wild rice kernel is a cereal grain produced from the annual water grass plant and is one of only two cereal grains native to North America. And, it is a requisite starch for a Minnesota hotdish.

This hotdish is a hearty winter meal to share with your family on your own dinner table. Try it with diced cooked chicken instead of beef or even Italian sausage. Hot dish is just a formula after all.

This recipe is my mom's handwritten formula for her wild rice hotdish.

---

1. Preheat oven to 350°F.
2. Combine brown rice and wild rice in a strainer and run cold water over to wash thoroughly.
3. In a medium saucepan, bring 2 cups of water to a boil. Add rice to boiling water. Add a pinch of salt.
4. Reduce heat to low and simmer covered for 35-50 minutes or just until the kernels puff to open.
5. Uncover, fluff with a fork and simmer for an additional 5 minutes. Drain any excess liquid. Do not overcook - the rice will finish cooking in the oven at the end.
6. In a cast iron skillet, sauté the ground beef, mushrooms, celery, and onions in butter.
7. Combine rice, ground beef mixture, soy sauce, sour cream and soup in a large bowl. Stir to combine. Season with pepper and salt (if desired). Add a splash of milk or two to the mix (or more sour cream), if the mixture seems too dry to heat in the oven.
8. Bake for about an hour, uncovered. Garnish with almonds and parsley.

1 cup brown rice
1 cup wild rice
4 cups water
pinch salt
1 ½ pounds ground beef
1 4-ounce can of mushrooms, drained
½ cup chopped celery
1 cup chopped onions
½ cup butter
¼ cup soy sauce
2 cups sour cream
1 10 ½-ounce can cream of mushroom soup
¼ teaspoon pepper
2 teaspoons salt (optional)
milk, as needed
parsley, minced, for garnish
½ cup slivered almonds, for garnish

# LASAGNA  *serves 16*

Another classic comfort food from my childhood was lasagna. This was definitely a much-loved dish then, and now.

Mom made her sauce from scratch. You can substitute your favorite jarred sauce, if you'd like to save time, but there is something extra special when you simmer the sauce all day. You can decide if you want your sauce to be chunky or smooth depending upon the type of canned tomatoes you use. Mom's sauce was chunky as she made it with canned tomatoes from our garden, whenever she had them in the pantry.

One thing I don't remember from my childhood was no-bake lasagna noodles. I love these! They save so much time and hassle. Even better? Pick a package of fresh lasagna noodles from your local Italian market. They take it to the next level!

I also discovered Ricotta cheese in college, which you can use instead of cottage cheese, if preferred. This small-town girl learned a lot when she ventured out. Cottage cheese was a low cost and available option in rural Minnesota. Mom had it on hand at all times. We used what we had and stocked items that served multiple purposes.

The original recipe below calls for quite a bit of vegetable oil so you can reduce it down to a couple of tablespoons. I prefer olive or avocado oil nowadays, but vegetable oil was the pantry staple on the farm back in the day. Feel free to adjust the amount and the type to your own personal preference.

---

- 4 quarts canned tomatoes
- 3 teaspoons (slightly heaping) oregano
- ¼ teaspoon pepper
- 2 teaspoons onion salt (substitute 1 teaspoon salt plus 1 teaspoon onion powder)
- 2 cups minced onions, or more
- 2 cloves garlic, minced
- ⅓ cup vegetable oil
- 3 pounds hamburger (ground beef)
- 2 teaspoons salt
- 2 16-ounce boxes of lasagna noodles
- 2 24-ounce packages of cottage cheese
- 8 ounces of grated parmesan cheese
- 16 ounces of mozzarella cheese, shredded
- 24 ounces of colby cheese, shredded

1. In a Dutch oven, combine tomatoes, salt, oregano, pepper and onion salt. Simmer.
2. In a skillet, sauté onions and garlic in vegetable oil. Add hamburger and brown until meat loses its red color.
3. Reserve about 4 cups of sauce and add to a small saucepan and continue to simmer on low. Add hamburger mixture to remaining tomato sauce in the Dutch oven and simmer for 2 ½ hours or until thickened, the longer the better.
4. Preheat oven to 350°F.
5. Cook lasagna noodles. Drain and separate.
6. Mix cottage cheese and parmesan cheese in a bowl. In a large bowl, mix together mozzarella and colby cheese.

7. In the bottom of a lasagna pan, spoon about 1 cup of the reserved tomato sauce to the pan and spread to cover the bottom of the pan. Layer a set of noodles lengthwise and then add another layer crosswise on top of the first layer. Cover the noodles with a layer of the meat sauce. Then add a layer of the cottage cheese and Parmesan mixture. Top with a layer of mozzarella and colby cheese mix.
8. Add another layer of lasagna noodles and repeat. End with more of the reserved tomato sauce and mozzarella and colby cheese. Repeat with a second pan.
9. Bake until bubbly, about 1 hour. Once the cheese starts to turn golden brown, gently place a tented piece of tin foil over the top to avoid burning the cheese.
10. Let stand for 15 minutes before serving.

*Tidbits from Jen's Kitchen*

This recipe makes enough for 2 lasagna pans. When it comes to making lasagna, I consider a lasagna pan essential. A lasagna pan is larger and deeper than most standard 9x13-inch cake pans and is made of a material that will conduct the heat evenly throughout the pan. You can use a cake pan if you don't have a lasagna pan, but you may end up with up to 3 pans of lasagna from the recipe below!

**Megan's Recipe Secret:**

I don't remember ever trying Sloppy Joes as a kid. This recipe was fun to try for the first time. I used homemade ketchup and dijon mustard (instead of yellow). I will definitely make this again!

# LOOSE MEAT SANDWICHES

*serves 6*

Ever heard of a loose meat sandwich? Depending upon where you grew up in the Midwest you might call it a Sloppy Joe, a Maid-Rite, a Manwich or just simply a loose meat sandwich.

While attending college at the University of Iowa, I discovered the Iowa version called a Made-Rite. It is the simplest form of this classic sandwich. A Made-Rite is merely minced onions and ground beef, simmered in chicken or beef broth until reduced. It is finished by swirling in a squirt or two of mustard at the very end.

The Sloppy Joe takes the simplicity of the Made-Rite up a notch and starts to add in vegetables and seasonings. I don't recall that we really had a family "recipe" for Sloppy Joes. We just went with what we had on hand and added in a long, healthy squeeze from the ketchup bottle along with a spoonful or two of brown sugar.

I also learned in college you could buy Sloppy Joe mix in a can! Who knew? But why on earth would you want to buy it from a can when you can make it just the way you like from scratch?

This adaptation from my recipe archives mirrors my childhood memories of that ever-so-messy sandwich, the Sloppy Joe. After living in Iowa for a few years, I definitely recommend a healthy squirt or two of yellow mustard to any variation of the loose meat sandwich.

---

1. In a small bowl, mix together ketchup and brown sugar until sugar is dissolved; set aside.
2. In a large skillet, brown meat together with peppers, garlic, onions, chili powder and oregano. Drain excess fat from the meat and vegetables using a colander; return to the skillet.
3. Add ketchup mixture and stir to combine. Cook over medium heat for 10 to 15 minutes. Just before serving, add a healthy squirt or two of yellow mustard.
4. Serve on buns.

**1 cup ketchup**
**1 tablespoon brown sugar**
**1 ½ pounds ground beef**
**½ cup chopped green bell peppers**
**3 cloves garlic, diced**
**1 cup chopped yellow onions**
**1-2 tablespoons chili powder**
**1 teaspoon dried oregano**
**a squirt or two of yellow mustard, to taste (optional, but highly recommended)**

OUR FARMHOUSE TABLE

# CHEESY HAM AND POTATOES *serves 4*

What do you do with leftover ham from the holidays? Cheesy ham and potatoes! This recipe was one of the very first recipes that I made as a young wife and mother. It may be one of the most requested "please will you make" recipes of my early years of adulting.

I think Mom must have been speaking from experience when she suggested not using Tupperware to shake the milk and flour mixture. You'll have to ask her yourself to confirm or deny how she learned of this tip!

---

**2 large potatoes, peeled and diced in ¾-1-inch cubes**
**¾-1 cup cubed ham (depending on the size of your potatoes)**
**2 cups milk**
**1 tablespoon butter**
**3 tablespoons flour**
**4 slices Velveeta cheese, cut at least ¼-inch thick**
**pinch of sugar**
**pepper, to taste**
**garlic powder, to taste**

1. In a medium saucepan, cook potatoes in salted water. Remove the potatoes, reserving cooking liquid.
2. Add butter to the same pan. Melt.
3. Combine milk, flour and seasonings. Shake in a mason glass jar with a lid as Tupperware explodes if you shake it too hard (and makes a mess).
4. Add milk mixture to butter. Stir with a whisk until thickened on medium heat. Add cheese, potatoes and ham. Season with sugar, pepper, and garlic powder, to taste.
5. Simmer on low for 10 to 15 minutes to allow flavors to blend.

### Tidbits from Jen's Kitchen

There was always a loaf of Velveeta around the house. If you are not a fan of Velveeta, then you can use American cheese, shredded from a block.

**Megan's Recipe Secret:**

I love this recipe a lot! I make it often in the winter, sometimes as a side dish without the ham. Other variations I have experimented with include using root veggies like turnips or rutabaga or cheddar and gouda instead of Velveeta.

**Megan's Recipe Secret:**

I make this Chop Suey with rice. In the summer, add baby bok choy when it is plentiful at the local farmers markets. I also love using tofu as the protein to soak up the flavors in the dish.

# CHOW MEIN (CHOP SUEY)

*serves 8*

We had a Chinese restaurant in Breckenridge that Mom and I liked to stop at for lunch when we were in town running the weekly errands. This was the extent of my exposure to international and ethnic cuisine. It was the 1970s and 1980s. This is just the way it was during that era in most Minnesota rural areas.

Beyond that, Mom would prepare a big batch of Chow Mein at home. Her recipe called for cubed pork, but you can also make it with diced chicken breast or chicken thighs. Mom's version is actually a bit more of a Chop Suey than Chow Mein as there are no noodles. Chop Suey is an American dish created in a Chinese style while Chow Mein is a more authentic Chinese dish.

---

1. In a large soup pot, sauté onion, celery and green pepper in butter with 1 tablespoon of water. Remove vegetables from the pot and set aside.
2. Brown pork or chicken in the soup pot next. Pour off any grease, if needed.
3. Add in soy sauce, salt, water and sprouts with their juice. Add in reserved vegetables. Stir to combine. Bring to a simmer over medium heat.
4. In a small bowl, mix cornstarch, sugar and water. Slowly add the cornstarch mixture to the soup pot, stirring constantly to avoid clumps. Simmer until the sauce thickens. Do not allow it to boil once the cornstarch has been added; adjust heat down, as needed.

1 ½ large onions, chopped
5 stalks celery, diced
1 green pepper, diced
1 tablespoon butter
1 pound of pork or chicken, cubed
4 tablespoons soy sauce
½ teaspoon salt, or to taste
4 cups water
3 14 ½-ounce cans bean sprouts with juice
7 tablespoons cornstarch
¼ teaspoon sugar
1 tablespoon brown sugar
¼ cup cold water

**Tidbits from Jen's Kitchen**

Feel free to adapt this mild base recipe and add in your own flair as I do. I like to add a couple cloves of minced garlic and 1-2 teaspoons of grated ginger to the vegetable mixture. You can also toss in a few sliced fresh mushrooms or shredded carrots with the onions, celery and peppers. To deepen the flavor profile further, I'll add 1 tablespoon of oyster sauce and 1-2 teaspoons of sesame oil with the soy sauce. You can toss in some cooked chow mein noodles at the end for a more authentic chow mein style dish.

# CORN-CROWNED PORK CHOPS *serves 2*

I'll be honest, as a child, pork chops were not my favorite dinner. They may have even been my very least favorite. Back then, pork chops were cut thin and were cooked well-done. While living in Iowa, I learned of the thick-cut Iowa pork chop, which changed my whole view on this cut of meat.

This is my mom's recipe for an oven-baked version. The corn "crust" helps keep the pork chops moist. You could also use this corn crust to coat chicken for a change of pace from traditional breaded chicken.

---

- 1 tablespoon butter
- 2 pork chops, thick cut
- 1 14 ¼-ounce can cream-style corn
- 1 large egg
- 1 large onion, diced fine
- 1 cup seasoned croutons (or bread cubes)

1. Preheat oven to 350°F.
2. In an oven-proof skillet with a cover, brown the pork chops on both sides in 1 tablespoon of butter. Set aside. Sauté onion in the same pan.
3. In a medium bowl, beat egg; add corn and season with salt and pepper, to taste. Stir in sautéed onion and bread cubes.
4. Place pork chops back into skillet; mound with a generous scoop of corn dressing on top of each of the chops.
5. Cover the skillet and bake for up to 1 hour. Let rest for 5 minutes before serving.

**Tidbits from Jen's Kitchen**

The cooking time listed is the original cooking time. Depending upon the size and thickness of your pork chops, you may need less cooking time. Check after 30 to 40 minutes. Insert a meat thermometer into the thickest part of the chops. For medium rare, pull from the oven when the pork chops reach 135°F and let rest until they reach 145°F. From medium, bake until the internal temperature is closer to 140°F and let rest until the pork chops reach 150°F.

**Megan's Recipe Secret:**

Instead of canned, I used the creamed corn from the recipe on Page 215.

# CANDIED CARROTS

*serves 6*

Dinners at the farmhouse table typically consisted of meat, potatoes and a vegetable. In the summer when produce was plentiful from the garden, we would have green beans, carrots, tomatoes or Minnesota sweet corn. Mom would often make candied carrots. I don't think there was really an official recipe, or at least I don't have a copy.

I mainly remember Mom's using butter and brown sugar. The one I have included in this collection is my adaptation of the recipe we practiced with in my culinary courses at the Art Institute in Virginia Beach. It has the classic sweet flavor of mom's but with nice tang from the orange juice and a little kick from the ginger.

---

1. Bring stock and orange juice to a boil in a large skillet. Add carrots, butter, sugar and maple syrup.
2. Stirring to coat carrots. Add ginger, to taste.
3. Simmer over medium heat, stirring constantly, until carrots are tender, about 10-15 minutes. Carrots should be tender when pierced with a fork.
4. Season to taste with salt and white pepper.

**3 tablespoons stock (vegetable or chicken)**
**3 tablespoons orange juice**
**1.5 pounds of carrots, cut into ½-inch x 2-inch sticks (about 3 ½ cups)**
**6 tablespoons cold butter**
**½ cup dark brown sugar**
**¼ cup of maple syrup**
**pinch of ground ginger, or more, to taste**
**salt, to taste**
**white pepper, to taste**

# GREEN BEAN CASSEROLE

*serves 6*

Green beans from the garden made a frequent appearance on the summertime table at the farm. Oftentimes, the vegetables we had for dinner were simply prepared and simmered on the stove top, especially during the week.

During the winter, when fresh vegetables were not available, we resorted to canned or frozen vegetables to bridge us through. Winter holidays frequently included this now classic casserole which originated in the 1950s with pantry staples from the era - canned green beans, mushroom soup and French-fried onions.

---

1 10 ½-ounce can of cream of mushroom soup
¾ cup milk
pinch of black pepper
2 14 ½-ounce cans French-style green beans, drained
1 ⅓ cups French-fried onions

1. Preheat oven to 350°F.
2. Mix soup, milk and pepper in a 1 ½-quart baking dish. Stir in beans and ⅔ cup fried onions.
3. Bake for 30 minutes or until hot. Stir.
4. Top with remaining ⅔ cup onions.
5. Bake for 5 minutes until onions are golden brown.

### Tidbits from Jen's Kitchen

To feed a crowd, double the recipe and prepare in a 9x13-inch baking dish. Use the entire 6-ounce container of onions, reserving 1 ⅓ cup for the topping. Increase initial cooking time to 40 minutes or until heated through. Top with onions and continue baking as described above.

**Megan's Recipe Secret:**

I use fresh or frozen green beans in this recipe instead of canned. I also like to make my cream of mushroom from scratch. First saute fresh mushrooms in butter. Then add flour to make a roux. Add milk or cream, season with onion and garlic powder, salt, and pepper. You just need enough milk to get to your desired consistency. Now you have your own home-made condensed cream of mushroom base for recipes!

# SWEET POTATOES

*serves 8*

Thanksgiving meant turkey, mashed potatoes with gravy and sweet potatoes. This recipe is for the traditional sweet potato dish with its gooey marshmallow topping that appeared on our dining room table at many Thanksgiving dinners.

---

1. Heat oven to 350°F. Grease a 9x13-inch glass baking dish.
2. Place sweet potatoes in the baking dish. Pour butter over potatoes. Sprinkle the sweet potatoes with brown sugar and salt. Top with marshmallows.
3. Bake for 25 to 30 minutes or until potatoes are thoroughly heated and marshmallows are lightly browned.

3 15-ounce cans sweet potatoes, canned
¼ cup butter, melted
½ cup firm packed brown sugar
½ teaspoon salt
marshmallows

**Tidbits from Jen's Kitchen**

Fresh sweet potatoes can be used instead of canned, which I definitely prefer. To use fresh sweet potatoes, place peeled sweet potatoes, cut into large chunks in a large saucepan or Dutch oven; cover with water. Bring to a boil. Reduce heat; cover and cook for 25-40 minutes or until just fork tender. Drain; cool slightly.

OUR FARMHOUSE TABLE

# PAN GRAVY *serves 6*

When Mom would prepare a beef or pork roast or whole chicken, gravy was a must to slather over the top of our meat and potatoes. Mom didn't use a recipe for gravy, it was just something she had done for so long by memory. She'd pull out a quart-size canning jar with a lid to shake the flour and milk. And, I do mean she shook it hard! Vigorously, you might say.

My first-time cooking Thanksgiving dinner, I didn't have her gravy formula written down. I was certainly not going to guess. I needed to find a formula. I turned to my cookbooks and through trial and error, came up with the formula that I now like best. This is my go-to base, adapted from Ina Garten's. The original recipe was published in "Barefoot Contessa, Family Style."

One modification I make to the original recipe is to strain out the onions from the pan juices in the pan. This pleases those who do not like a chunky gravy.

This recipe allows you to get the gravy started while your meat is roasting in the oven. You can make a delicious gravy without the pan juices. It can save you a lot of time allowing the meal to come together more easily. Use a high quality chicken stock for best results. You can even make the gravy the day before!

The formula also works well for a beef or pork roast. You can use beef or chicken stock along with any pan juices. For beef, use red wine and brandy instead of white wine and cognac.

---

1 stick butter, unsalted
1 medium sweet onion, preferably a sweet Vidalia, minced or grated
¼ cup flour (or more as needed)
salt, to taste
¼ teaspoon white pepper
1 cup chicken stock
1 cup pan juices (from turkey, chicken or game hens or additional stock)
1 tablespoon heavy cream
1 tablespoon dry white wine, preferably Sauvignon Blanc
2 teaspoons cognac, optional

1. In a large skillet, cook the butter and onion over medium heat until the onions are lightly browned and starting to caramelize.
2. Add flour and whisk to combine. Season with salt and pepper. Cook for 3-5 minutes. Add stock and pan juices and cook, whisking constantly, until thickened, about another 5 minutes.
3. Strain the mixture through a sieve or strainer with small holes. Return the gravy mixture to the skillet.
4. Whisk in cream, wine and cognac, if using. Simmer for another 2-3 minutes to allow flavors to meld.

*Tidbits from Jen's Kitchen*

If you love onions, then skip Step 3. Instead use an immersion blender to blend the onions into the gravy for a smooth, flavor-packed version. Continue on with Step 4 to finish.

# CHEESE SAUCE

*serves 8*

Megan asked me why there were not more vegetable recipes when we were compiling the list for this collection. Vegetables on the farmhouse table most nights were quite simple. That was my answer.

Some nights, vegetables were "dressed up" with Velveeta cheese. Mom would place a slice or two over broccoli or cauliflower and let it melt just enough before serving. She would also make a cheese sauce with milk on occasion. It was not a recipe that she ever wrote down. This version comes pretty close to my mom's.

Velveeta was quite the invention for a farmhouse cook, especially in rural Minnesota. Just think, you could buy it ahead and not have to refrigerate it. Cheese available any time, without going bad. Mom always had a box or two in the pantry in reserve.

---

1. In a small saucepan over medium-low heat, combine cheese and milk. Start with about ¼ cup of milk and then add more, as needed.
2. Whisk until smooth, stirring constantly. Add seasonings.
3. Continue to simmer until thickened, stirring occasionally.

**Velveeta chunks (about 1 cup of chunks)**
**¼-½ cup milk (enough to thin the cheese)**
**½ teaspoon garlic powder**
**½ teaspoon salt, or to taste**
**pinch of pepper, or to taste**

**Tidbits from Jen's Kitchen**

I have adapted Mom's basic sauce into my own, made from scratch variation. It starts with a roux (2 tablespoons butter and flour) and use freshly shredded cheese from the block to finish. Add a splash or two of milk to thin, as needed. You can use about any cheese in place of Velveeta, but I find that shredded American and Swiss cheese are my two favorites. They keep the texture creamy and smooth like Mom's Velveeta cheese sauce. When I make it with Swiss cheese, I dress it up a bit by adding 1/4 cup of white wine to finish it off.

*cheese sauce*

OUR FARMHOUSE TABLE

# SPAGHETTI SAUCE

*serves 4*

Italian night on the farm was either spaghetti or lasagna. Mom would make her own spaghetti sauce from scratch with canned tomatoes preserved from the garden.

The longer you simmer it, the better it tastes. Simmering concentrates the flavors and brings out sweetness by breaking down carbohydrates, creating that caramelized flavor of a deep, rich pasta sauce. This recipe is a one-pot version that simmers the meat and tomatoes together instead of simmering the sauce then adding the meat later.

---

1 1/4 pounds ground beef (or sausage)
1 cup diced onions
4 tablespoons butter, or less to taste
4 teaspoons garlic salt*
1 ½ quarts tomato sauce
1 ½ teaspoons brown sugar, packed and heaping
3 teaspoons dried basil
1 teaspoon salt, or less to taste
1/4 teaspoon pepper
1 cup grated parmesan cheese, divided
spaghetti noodles, cooked according to package directions

1. In a large cast iron skillet, brown onions and ground beef in butter and garlic salt.
2. Add tomatoes, brown sugar and basil, stirring to combine. Season salt and pepper, to taste.
3. Add ½ cup parmesan cheese (or a parmesan rind, if you have one) to the sauce and stir to combine.
4. Simmer for at least 20 minutes, the longer the better.
5. Serve over cooked spaghetti noodles. Garnish with remaining parmesan cheese.

**Tidbits from Jen's Kitchen**

You may be thinking, wow, 4 teaspoons of garlic salt is a lot of garlic salt. I agree. I recommend cutting this back and using 1 teaspoon to start and then add more as it simmers to get the desired taste you prefer.

# EASY CORNBREAD
*serves 6*

Cornbread with maple syrup brings back fond memories for me – served hot with butter and warm maple syrup. Mom would also bake cornbread to serve with chili. Nothing goes better with chili than cornbread. So, is it breakfast or is it a dessert? I don't know but it is delicious!

You can certainly opt to buy cornbread mix in the box, but it is so easy to bake up a batch from scratch with just a few ingredients. You likely already have them on hand in your pantry.

---

1. Grease a cast iron skillet or 8-inch square baking dish with butter. Heat oven to 400°F, if using a metal pan or cast iron skillet, or 375°F for a glass dish.
2. In a large bowl, combine all dry ingredients. Stir in the milk, oil and egg, mixing just until dry ingredients are moistened. Do not over mix.
3. Pour batter into a greased pan or skillet. Bake for 20-25 minutes or until golden brown and a wooden toothpick inserted near the center comes out clean.
4. Serve warm.

1 ¼ cups flour
¾ cup cornmeal
¼ cup sugar
2 teaspoons baking powder
½ teaspoon salt (optional)
1 cup skim milk
¼ cup vegetable oil
2 egg whites or 1 large egg, beaten

**Tidbits from Jen's Kitchen**

Mom's recipe is a sweeter take on cornbread, a great breakfast version. If you like yours a little less sweet, you can take the sugar down to ⅛ cup. Low fat buttermilk can also be used instead of skim milk, as I do.

I love to bake cornbread in a cast iron skillet. The edges turn out nice and crispy and the skillet makes for fun presentation.

# PIZZA DOUGH

Take out or pizza delivery? Nah, we didn't have that growing up at our farm 20 miles from town. Dine in or carry-out pizza? Only Pizza Hut that I recall. I sadly learned that our local hometown Pizza Hut closed in 2020. It was one of my favorite hang-out joints in high school once I could drive.

Our family made pizza at home. My memory of pizza nights centered around dinners where Dad was the chef for the night. He would take out a frozen Red Baron or Tombstone and proceed to doctor it up with more cheese than you can imagine. He would then top with additional ground beef or sausage. There was a mountain of toppings on that pizza when it was placed in the oven. The crust was just the humble carrier.

If one of us women were in charge, we made homemade pizza with a scratch-made crust. This is the version I still use from my recipe box.

**1 cups flour**
**½ cup warm water**
**1 ½ teaspoons yeast**
**1 tablespoon shortening**
**¾ teaspoon salt**

1. Combine ½ cup flour, yeast and salt in a medium bowl. Mix well. Add water and shortening. Mix with a spoon until somewhat smooth. Do not over mix.
2. Gradually stir in remaining flour to make a stiff dough.
3. Let rest for 15 minutes. Preheat oven to 400°F.
4. Spread out on a cookie sheet. Pinch edges.
5. Top with your favorite pizza sauce and toppings.
6. Bake for 25-30 minutes or until golden and crispy on the edges.

**Megan's Recipe Secret:**

I love adding garlic powder or dried herbs to my pizza dough for extra flavor! To avoid large bubbles in the crust, lightly poke the fork around the dough before adding pizza sauce.

# Sweet Treats & Baked Desserts

*Kenny celebrating the big "50"!*         *Jenny turns two!*

I loved to bake at a very early age. My mom taught me how to read a recipe about the same time I was learning to read books. I baked my first cake standing on a kitchen chair as I was not tall enough to reach the countertop yet. From that moment on, I would spend summers baking sweet treats and baked goodies to share with our family and neighbors, but even more importantly, for my dad to enjoy while in the field. Farming was hard work with long days. It made me so happy when he would share one of my homemade treats with a neighbor or another farmer, telling them with pride "Look what my little girl baked today!"

Truly, baking from scratch is not as hard as you may think. You just need a good recipe and then follow the directions. It is really no more work than whipping something up from a box mix. What is different? The texture and flavor of a home baked treat are superior to anything from a box. The farm pantry, refrigerator and freezer were always stocked with the essential ingredients necessary to bake. Not only flour, butter and sugar, but chocolate chips, nuts and other goodies were on hand to make one of these recipes at a moment's notice.

My collection has far more recipes for cakes, bars, cookies and other desserts than anything else in my first recipe box. Each one has a delicious memory of its own.

# CARAMELITAS

*serves 24*

A family favorite that I have been baking since I was young...Sinfully decadent! This is Aunt Carolyn's recipe that she made for one family gathering or another, I am sure. It was then quickly added to our family recipe collection as a "keeper." Caramelitas made frequent appearances on the farm.

---

1. Melt caramels with milk in a double boiler. With a spatula, scrap into a bowl and set aside.
2. Melt chips and condensed milk in the double boiler. When melted, add nuts.
3. Preheat oven to 350°F.
4. Mix all remaining ingredients together to make the crumb crust. Press ⅔ of the crumbs into a greased 7x11-inch pan.
5. Bake for 10 minutes.
6. Cover crumb crust with melted caramels, then spread with chocolate mixture. Dot the top of the bars with the remaining crumb mixture.
7. Bake for 15 minutes or until the crumb topping is golden brown. Cool.
8. Cut these bars into small pieces as they are very rich!

32 caramels, unwrapped
5 tablespoons milk
4 ounces semi-sweet chocolate chips
½ can sweetened condensed milk
½ cup chopped walnuts or pecans
1 cup flour
1 cup quick oats
¾ cup brown sugar
½ teaspoon baking soda
¼ teaspoon salt
¾ cup melted margarine

SWEET TREATS AND DESSERTS

# CHOCOLATE BROWNIES

*serves 12*

Bars, or bar cookies as you may call them, are a potluck staple. Bar cookie batter is poured or pressed into a baking pan, baked, cooled and cut in "bars" - squares, rectangles or even diamonds. Essentially, cookie bars, like brownies and others featured in this section, take cookies to the next level. You can create layers of goodness on top of the cookie bar base.

This is my mom's recipe for brownies. It was one of the first recipes I learned to bake from scratch, and I have been baking these ever since. Aunt Carolyn's chocolate icing is amazing for the top. A brownie is not a brownie without that layer of fudgy icing on top.

---

- 2 large eggs, 3, if small
- 1 cup sugar
- ⅔ cup vegetable oil
- 4 tablespoons unsweetened cocoa
- 1 teaspoon vanilla extract
- 1 cup flour
- ¾ teaspoon salt
- ½ teaspoon baking powder
- ½ cup chopped pecans or walnuts (optional)

1. Preheat oven to 350°F. Grease a 7x11-inch pan.
2. In a large mixing bowl, beat eggs. Add sugar, oil, cocoa and vanilla.
3. Stir in flour, salt and baking powder. Mix to combine.
4. Stir in nuts, if using.
5. Bake for 15-17 minutes.

SWEET TREATS AND DESSERTS

# CHOCOLATE ICING

I can't even tell you how many pans of brownies were baked on the farm by my sister, my mom and I over the years. This is my favorite icing for brownies, another of Aunt Carolyn's recipes. An unfrosted brownie is naked, in my opinion. The bar is simply a carrier for this sinful goodness on top.

I remember when I was just out of college and working as an auditor, one of my friends, a coworker (who will remain nameless as she has since become a wonderful home chef) asked me to teach her how to bake. She wanted to bake a cake from scratch for her boyfriend with this frosting on top. It was his favorite. I gave her the recipe so she could shop for the ingredients and then I went over to her place so we could bake together. While the cake was baking, we started to prepare the icing. Much to my dismay, she only had spreadable margarine! I think it was Parkay or something similar. I said, "we shall see, but I don't think it will thicken." And it did not. What we had concocted was lovely chocolate sauce that was delicious when drizzled over an emergency scoop of vanilla ice cream atop each slice of cake. Her boyfriend was none the wiser.

Her first baking lesson was this: the first time you bake something, don't substitute ingredients and follow the recipe as described. From there, you can experiment and adjust to your own liking.

---

1. In a medium saucepan, stir ingredients together. Bring to a boil. Using a candy thermometer, bring temperature to 214°F in the middle. Boil for 1 minute and 20 seconds without stirring.
2. Makes enough for an 8x8-inch or 9x9-inch pan. For a cake, make 1 ½ times the recipe. For a large sheet pan of brownies, make a double batch.

1 cup sugar
¼ cup butter or margarine
¼ cup milk
½ cup unsweetened cocoa

SWEET TREATS AND DESSERTS

# FUDGE NUT BARS

*makes 48 bars*

If you asked me which of the bar recipes included in this book was my favorite, I really would have a hard time picking one. Fudge nut bars would definitely be a front runner. There is something about the combination of the fudge nut center surrounded by the oatmeal crust and topping. You can choose nearly any nut for this recipe. We usually made them with walnuts or pecans, but peanuts or cashews are tasty alternatives.

---

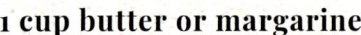

1 cup butter or margarine
2 cups light brown sugar
2 large eggs
2 teaspoons vanilla extract
2 ½ cups flour
1 teaspoon baking soda
1 teaspoon salt
3 cups rolled oats, uncooked, quick cooking
12 ounces milk chocolate chips
1 cup sweetened condensed milk
2 tablespoons butter
½ teaspoon salt
2 teaspoons vanilla extract
1 cup chopped nuts, pecans or walnuts

1. Preheat oven to 350°F.
2. In a stand mixer, cream together butter and sugar on medium speed. Add eggs and vanilla, mix to combine. Add in flour, baking soda, salt and rolled oats. Mix on low speed until combined. Set aside while you make the filling.
3. In a double boiler, mix together chocolate chips, sweetened condensed milk, butter and salt. Stir until mixture is smooth. Stir in nuts and vanilla.
4. Spread two-thirds of the oatmeal mixture in the bottom of a greased jelly roll pan. Cover with chocolate mixture. Dot with remaining oatmeal topping.
5. Bake at 350°F for 20-30 minutes.

**Tidbits from Jen's Kitchen**

If you don't have a double boiler, don't let that scare you away from trying this yummy recipe. I don't own one anymore. If you don't have one, you can set a stainless steel mixing bowl over a pan of water instead.

You also may be thinking to yourself, what is a jelly roll pan? A jelly-roll pan is either 15 ½x10 ½-inches or 18x12-inches, has 1-inch-high sides and is perfect for making cake rolls and cookie bars. It is also referred to as a half sheet pan.

# SWEETENED CONDENSED MILK

A well-stocked pantry was essential growing up on the farm. We were 20 miles away from the nearest small town with a grocery store. But even then, you sometimes needed to improvise when you ran out of ingredients. This sweetened condensed milk is such a recipe. We could always pull out the recipe and make a batch for those emergency situations when we didn't have the canned version around.

1. Place warm water in a bowl set over a pan of hot water.
2. Add dry milk and mix well.
3. Add sugar and mix well, until smooth.

½ cup warm water
½ cup plus 2 tablespoons dry milk powder
¾ cup sugar

# O'HENRY BARS

*makes 48 bars*

O'Henry Bars are another front runner for best bar recipe, in my opinion. This bar is inspired by the O'Henry candy bar, which dates back to the 1920s. The candy bar is made of peanuts, caramel, and fudge that is coated in milk chocolate.

I love anything with peanut butter and chocolate. Enjoying one of these tasty bars as a child is likely when I first discovered this fact. There is something about the gooey oat layer topped with creamy, peanut buttery, milk chocolate.

The original family recipe used vegetable oil, but I prefer to use a full fat high quality butter instead of oil. Take them to the next level by sprinkling with flake sea salt. The salt nicely cuts the sweetness of the bar and adds a bit of a crunch too.

---

**1 ½ cups vegetable oil**
**2 cups brown sugar**
**1 cup corn syrup, light or dark**
**6 teaspoons vanilla extract**
**1 teaspoon salt**
**8 cups rolled oats, uncooked, old fashioned**
**2 cups milk chocolate chips, melted**
**1 cup peanut butter**

1. Preheat oven to 370°F.
2. Mix oil, sugar, corn syrup, vanilla and salt in a large bowl. Fold in rolled oats.
3. Press mixtures into a greased bar jelly roll or sheet pan.
4. Bake for 12 minutes. Cool.
5. Mix together melted chocolate chips (using a double boiler) and peanut butter. Spread over the baked layer.
6. Allow the chocolate topping set before cutting into bars.

# LEMON BARS
*makes 36 bars*

My mom has been making these bars for as long as I can remember. To this day, it is one of Mom's top five most likely bars or cookies to have on hand for visitors. They are sweet and tart at the same time. The buttery crust contrasts nicely with the lemon layer.

You may have noticed in some recipes there are two different temperatures listed depending upon what type of pan you are using: metal or glass. Pyrex glass bakeware was an invention of the early 1900s and its popularity increased over the years as it became more affordable. Pyrex, now a household name brand, was like no other bakeware back in the day. It could withstand temperature changes (bake, refrigerate and freeze in the same dish). It didn't discolor or react with ingredients nor did it absorb food smells. If you had one of their see-through pieces, you could now watch your baked goods turn golden brown quite easily.

With invention comes adaptation. Glassware bakes differently than metal or ceramic. Most of our family recipes were historically made in aluminum or other metal pans. They now required an adjustment to the temperatures. The rule of thumb for baking in glass is to lower the oven temperature by 25°F from what the original recipe calls for. You may also need to add up to 10 minutes to the baking time.

---

1. Preheat oven to 350°F (or 325°F for a glass pan).
2. In a medium bowl, mix together the flour, sugar and butter. Pack into the bottom of a jelly roll pan or pack two-thirds of the dough into a 9x13-inch pan and then the rest into an 8x8-inch pan. Bake for 15-20 minutes.
3. In a large bowl, beat together all of the topping ingredients. Pour over the crust. Bake for 15-20 minutes. If the custard is browned but not fully thickened, turn the oven down to warm until the custard sets.
4. Dust with powdered sugar while hot.
5. Run a knife around the edges immediately to make it easier to remove from the plan. Cool.
6. Freeze for an hour to firm the bars up for easier cutting. Cut into squares.

**Crust:**
2 cups flour
½ cup powdered sugar
1 cup butter or margarine

**Topping:**
8 eggs
3 cups sugar
1 ½ teaspoon baking powder
3/4 teaspoon salt
½ cup lemon juice
3 tablespoons grated lemon peel

powdered sugar, for garnish

**Tidbits from Jen's Kitchen**

I typically start with the original baking time and then see if it needs to remain in longer. I also check my baked goods about 5 minutes before the recommended baking time, as every oven is different. You can always leave your baked goods in for more time, but there is not much you can do if you overbake something.

# MY FAVORITE CHOCOLATE CAKE
*serves 12*

This was the first cake that I learned to bake from scratch. It is moist and chocolatey and pairs so well with cream cheese frosting. You can also turn it into a German-chocolate style cake by topping with the coconut pecan frosting included in this collection.

---

- 1 teaspoon baking soda
- ½ cup unsweetened cocoa
- 1 cup boiling water
- ⅔ cup vegetable oil
- 2 cups sugar
- 2 large or 3 medium eggs
- 3 cups flour
- 1 cup sour cream (in a pinch, substitute soured milk - 1 cup milk plus 1 tablespoon vinegar)
- 1 teaspoon vanilla extract
- ½ teaspoon salt

1. Preheat oven to 350°F. Grease a 9x13-inch cake pan and set aside.
2. Mix baking soda and cocoa in a bowl. Pour boiling water over the mixture and stir to combine. Set aside.
3. In the bowl of a stand mixer, combine oil and sugar. Blend on medium speed until light and fluffy. Add eggs and mix until incorporated. Add flour slowly, ½ cup at a time, mixing on low speed until combined. Add sour cream (or sour milk). Slowly pour in chocolate mixture, stirring on low until incorporated. Add vanilla and salt and stir until combined.
4. Pour into a greased 9x13-inch cake pan and bake for 30-40 minutes, or until a toothpick inserted into the center comes out clean.

### Tidbits from Jen's Kitchen

We did not have sour cream on hand very often, so we used the "in a pinch" method substituting milk and vinegar frequently. It was my sister, Rebecca, who uncovered the fact that using sour cream is a worthy investment. The milk and vinegar option should be reserved for when you are truly in a pinch.

# COCONUT PECAN FROSTING *yields 2 1/2 cups*

The other way I liked to frost a sour cream chocolate cake is with this coconut pecan frosting, creating a German Chocolate-style variation. You can also use it as the filling for a layer cake and then frost with vanilla cream cheese frosting sprinkled with chopped pecans and toasted coconut.

1. Combine milk, sugar, eggs, butter and vanilla in a saucepan and cook over medium heat, stirring until thickened, about 12 minutes.
2. Stir in coconut and pecans.
3. Cool until thick enough to spread, beating occasionally with a whisk.

1 cup evaporated milk
1 cup sugar
3 large egg yolks, slightly beaten
½ cup butter
1 teaspoon vanilla extract
1 ⅓ cups flaked coconut
1 cup chopped pecans

*coconut pecan frosting*

# CREAM CHEESE FROSTING
*2 layer or 9x13*

Aunt Irene's recipe for cream cheese frosting was one of a handful of "go-to" frosting recipes we made frequently on the farm. Cream cheese frosting is hard to beat! It is still my choice for frosting a chocolate cake.

Cream cheese frosting is a variation on a buttercream, which is my husband Jamie's favorite frosting. You would think growing up on a Midwestern farm that buttercream frosting would be the standard. It was not. Cream cheese was our preferred frosting election. I was a child of the 1970s and cream cheese frosting was a newer "invention" back then. It only started to become popular in the 1960s, as cream cheese became more widely available.

Traditionally, cream cheese frosting is the choice for red velvet, carrot and spice cakes but we used it for just about any cake by simply varying the flavoring. Think of all the variations that you could do! Flavor your base frosting with maple syrup or orange peel instead of vanilla and lemon. Stir in some peanut butter and spread on your brownies sprinkled with crushed peanuts. The options are endless.

---

¼ pound butter or margarine
1 8-ounce package of cream cheese
1 teaspoon vanilla extract
¼-½ teaspoon lemon juice
2-3 cup powdered sugar

1. Allow cream cheese to come to room temperature.
2. In the bowl of your stand mixer, combine sugar and butter or margarine. Beat until creamy and lump-free.
3. Stir in vanilla extract and lemon juice.
4. With the mixer on Speed 1, add sugar gradually and stir to combine.
5. Increase speed slightly once all the sugar has been added until fully combined and smooth.

SWEET TREATS AND DESSERTS

**Megan's Recipe Secret:**

Substitute 1 tablespoon cocoa for lemon juice for a great chocolate frosting.

# EASY "YELLOW" CAKE
*serves 12*

All cakes start with the same basic ingredients: flour, sugar, a leavening agent, fat and eggs. The variations from there define the cake. I grew up thinking that this recipe was a "white" cake. It is more accurately described as a yellow cake as it includes the egg yolks. A true white cake in the pastry world includes only the whites. Yellow cake also uses butter or margarine as the fat instead of oil. The combination of the two creates the signature yellow color of the cake, while maintaining a neutral flavor. A yellow cake tastes more rich than white cake because of the egg yolks and choice of fat.

---

1. Preheat oven to 350°F (325°F for a glass baking dish). Grease a 9x13-inch cake pan and set aside.
2. In a large bowl by hand or with a stand mixer, beat eggs very well. Add sugar gradually. Beat.
3. Stir flour, baking powder and salt together in a small bowl. Then add slowly to eggs and sugar.
4. In a small saucepan, heat milk to warm and add margarine. Stir until melted. Add to the batter and mix to combine. Stir in vanilla.
5. Pour batter into your prepared cake pan.
6. Bake for 30 minutes. Reduce time to 25 minutes, if making a layer cake.

**4 large eggs**
**2 cups sugar**
**2 cups flour**
**2 teaspoons baking powder**
**½ teaspoon salt**
**1 cup milk, warmed**
**2 tablespoons margarine (or butter)**
**2 teaspoons vanilla extract**

*Tidbits from Jen's Kitchen*

This easy cake was often the base for birthday cakes on the farm. I love it topped with the cocoa variation of Irene's cream cheese frosting.

SWEET TREATS AND DESSERTS

# ANGEL FOOD CAKE

*serves 8*

Dad was the angel food cake baker and has been doing so since he was a child. This recipe was his mother's recipe. As the story goes, Dad would pick the eggs from the hen house each day. He may not have been on very good terms with the chickens because when he would reach into the coop to nab an egg from under the hens, they would start to peck him. If you have ever been pecked by a hen, then you will not be surprised by the fact Dad often ended up with a few cracked eggs. These eggs need to be used immediately. And, what better way to use them than an angel food cake?

As my dad was the youngest of the three brothers and second youngest of the seven, he spent time as a young boy in the kitchen with his mother and sisters where he learned to bake and to use up those cracked eggs! He would bring baked goods into Breckenridge to the local Stratford hotel, trading them for a hot meal at the hotel's restaurant.

Birthdays in the summer, like mine, meant Dad would bake you angel food cake. Angel food cake differs from other cakes because it uses no butter. Its aerated texture comes from whipped egg whites. An angel food cake brings back the fond memories of summer birthday parties with friends and family. Mom would serve us a lovely slice of angel food cake topped with a fresh fruit and a dollop of whipped cream. Sometimes, we would frost it with the soft frosting recipe included in this chapter.

1. Preheat oven to 375°F.
2. Whip egg whites until they are stiff with a stand mixer. Then add the cream of tartar and vanilla extract.
3. Increase speed to medium and continue whipping, adding sugar 1 tablespoon at a time. Wait 5-10 seconds between each addition to give time for the sugar to incorporate. Increase to medium-high speed and whip until it reaches stiff peaks.
4. Using a rubber spatula, gently fold the flour mixture into the egg whites ¼ cup at a time. Repeat until all the flour mixture has been added.
5. Pour the batter into the ungreased round angel food cake tube pan and smooth out the top with your rubber spatula. Then run a knife through the batter to break up any air bubbles. Run the knife around the outside wall and inside wall of the pan as well.
6. Bake until lightly golden on top and a toothpick inserted in the middle comes out clean, about 30 minutes.
7. Immediately after removing from the oven, turn the cake upside down to cool on the pan's feet.
8. Allow the cake to cool for about 1 hour.
9. Once cooled, turn it right side up and run a knife or spatula along the outside and inside walls of the pan to loosen it. Invert the cake onto a serving plate.
10. Top with soft frosting or powdered sugar. Slice the cake with a serrated knife and use a careful sawing motion. Any other knife will squish the cake and it won't look nearly as pretty.
11. Serve with fresh fruit and whipped cream.

**12 egg whites**
**1 teaspoon cream of tartar**
**1 teaspoon vanilla extract**
**1 ½ cups sugar, sifted 4 times**
**1 cup flour, sifted 4 times**
**Soft Frosting, if desired (Page 151)**
**fresh mixed berries**

*Tidbits from Jen's Kitchen*

Dad likes to set the cake pan on the neck of an empty glass soda or wine bottle to cool, ensuring the cake has lots of air flow around it.

SWEET TREATS AND DESSERTS

# SOFT FROSTING

If you were to top an angel food cake with a frosting, this was it. Its light cloud-like texture is heavenly when slathered on an angel food cake.

1. Beat egg whites until stiff.
2. Gradually add in powdered sugar and whip until a smooth, light frosting develops.
3. Add vanilla and gently fold with a rubber spatula to combine.
4. Double the recipe for a layer cake or an angel food cake.

**2 egg whites, beaten until stiff**
**1 cup powdered sugar**
**1 teaspoon vanilla extract**

***Tidbits from Jen's Kitchen***

When whipping egg whites, start out with room temperature egg whites and whip with a very clean bowl and whisk for the best result. Any residue on your bowl or whisk may result in egg whites that won't stiffen. Also, make sure you don't have any trace of egg yolks in your whites as the fat in the yolks will prevent the whites from stiffening. Fresh egg whites will also whip up more quickly and be more stable than older eggs. When whipping egg whites for a recipe, you must exercise patience. For soft peaks to form it will take several minutes. For stiff peaks, it will take another 2 to 3 minutes.

SWEET TREATS AND DESSERTS

# APPLESAUCE CAKE *serves 12*

This simple cake tastes like fall. It was not one we baked frequently. I am not sure why. It was delicious and never last long when we baked it.

---

1. Preheat oven to 350°F. Grease a 9x13-inch cake pan.
2. Cream butter and sugar in a stand mixer. Add eggs. Beat well. Add in applesauce and blend to combine. Slowly add flour, baking soda, cinnamon, nutmeg and clove. Mix to incorporate. Add lemon, vanilla and nuts, if desired, and stir to combine.
3. Bake for 30 minutes then lower heat to 300°F for 30 minutes, or until a toothpick inserted in the center comes out clean.

**2 cups sugar**
**1 ½ cups butter**
**3 large eggs**
**3 cups sweetened applesauce**
**4 cups flour**
**4 teaspoons baking soda**
**2 teaspoons cinnamon**
**1 teaspoon nutmeg**
**½ teaspoon cloves**
**2 teaspoons lemon juice**
**1 teaspoon vanilla extract**
**pecans or walnuts nuts, chopped, if desired**

**Megan's Recipe Secret:**

I used unsweetened applesauce. It is sweet enough for me!

# OATMEAL CRISPIES

*makes 60 cookies*

Selecting which cookie recipes to feature in this cookbook was hard. There were so many recipes to pick from! We baked dozens and dozens of cookies over the years. Oatmeal Crispies were a solid pick as they were crunchy on the edges and a bit soft in the middle.

---

1. Preheat oven to 350°F.
2. In a large bowl using a hand mixer, thoroughly cream margarine and sugar. Add eggs and vanilla. Beat well. Add dry ingredients and mix well. Stir in walnuts at the end. Shape into balls, place on a cookie sheet and then flatten.
3. Bake for 10 minutes at 350°F.

- 1 cup margarine or shortening
- 2 cups brown sugar
- 2 beaten large eggs
- 1 teaspoon vanilla extract
- 1 ½ cups flour
- 1 teaspoon salt
- 1 teaspoon baking powder
- 3 cups rolled oats, uncooked, old fashioned
- ½ cup chopped walnuts

SWEET TREATS AND DESSERTS

# PEANUT BUTTER COOKIES *makes 24 cookies*

I think I told you already that I love anything that is made with peanut butter, especially for dessert. Reese's peanut butter cups and Butterfingers are my favorite candy bars from my childhood, and still are to this day.

It only makes sense that my all-time favorite cookie was peanut butter. I can't even tell you how many times I have baked these cookies over the years. They are firm but tender and oh so good!

---

- 1 cup sugar
- 1 cup brown sugar
- 1 cup shortening
- 2 large eggs
- ¾ cup creamy peanut butter
- 1 teaspoon vanilla extract
- 3 cups flour
- ½ teaspoon salt
- 2 teaspoons baking soda

1. Preheat oven to 375°F.
2. Cream together shortening and sugars with either a hand mixer or a stand mixer. Add in eggs and blend. Stir in peanut butter and vanilla. Add flour, salt and baking soda to the batter and mix well.
3. Using a teaspoon, scoop out a small portion of dough. Roll gently with your hands into a ball. Place each ball on a cookie sheet. Flatten with a fork making a crisscross pattern on top.
4. Bake for 8-10 minutes, depending upon size. Don't over bake.

# GINGER SNAPS

*makes 24-36 cookies*

Ginger snaps bring back memories of the holidays. It was one of the many cookies we would bake and freeze ahead, stocking them up for the holiday season. We always had plenty of cookies on hand for entertaining, gift plates or to bring to family gatherings. My mom's ginger snaps were always crispy on the outside with soft centers. So good!

We baked a lot with shortening, or vegetable shortening. Prior to the invention of vegetable shortening, you would find older recipes called for lard. During the depression, vegetable shortening became popular as it was more readily available and cheaper than butter or lard. The key difference between butter and lard? Lard is 100% fat while butter contains about 18% water.

I don't usually keep shortening on hand nowadays. Coconut oil is my go-to fat for baking and is a great substitute for butter or shortening in most recipes.

---

1. Preheat oven to 350°F.
2. In a large bowl, mix eggs and molasses with 1 cup sugar and shortening. Cream with a handheld mixer. Add flour, baking soda, salt, ginger, cinnamon and cloves. Mix to combine.
3. Place remaining sugar in a small bowl. Roll portions of the dough into small balls and then flatten with a fork. Roll balls in sugar and place on a cookie sheet.
4. Bake for 7-8 minutes.

**¾ cup shortening**
**2 cup sugar, divided**
**1 large egg**
**4 tablespoons molasses**
**2 cups flour**
**3 teaspoons baking soda**
**¼ teaspoon salt**
**1 teaspoon ground ginger**
**1 teaspoon ground cinnamon**
**1 teaspoon ground cloves**

# MEXICAN WEDDING CAKES
*makes 48 cookies*

Mexican wedding cakes were another cookie Mom would bake for the holidays or special occasions. They are buttery little bite size cookies. They look so pretty and fancy but are simple to make.

You may find these similar to another recipe, Russian Tea cakes. Mexican wedding cakes traditionally use pecans as the nut while Russian Tea cakes use walnuts, almonds or hazelnuts.

---

½ cup butter, softened
½ cup shortening, softened
6 tablespoons powdered sugar
1 teaspoon vanilla extract
2 cups flour
1 cup finely chopped nuts
powdered sugar, for rolling

1. Preheat oven to 350°F.
2. Cream butter and shortening well in your stand mixer. Add sugar and blend. Then add remaining ingredients. Roll into small balls.
3. Bake for about 10 minutes.
4. Roll in powdered sugar while still warm.
5. Store overnight before serving.

**Megan's Recipe Secret:**

Figs make an excellent substitute for dates.

# GRANDMA'S PUMPKIN COOKIES
*makes 36 cookies*

These soft, cake-like cookies with a powdered sugar frosting are a recipe from my grandmother on my mom's side, Phyllis McKee. My mom would bake these in the fall and winter months. I know they were one of Megan's favorites as a child. Megan loved it when she would arrive at the lake cabin and her grandmother would offer her cookies almost immediately after walking in the door. What child wouldn't?

I don't recall Mom using the chopped dates in the recipe, but the original version from my grandmother calls for them. I like to add a bit of orange zest to frosting for added zip!

Mom would often use cooked squash in our garden in recipes that call for pumpkin. You'd never know the difference. We often had bumper crops of squash on the farm, which Mom would freeze in the fall for later use.

---

1. Preheat oven to 350°F.
2. In the bowl of a stand mixer, cream sugar and margarine. Add in pumpkin and egg(s). Then dry ingredients. Mix to combine. Add in nuts and dates, if using, and vanilla and stir to combine.
3. Drop from a spoon onto a cookie sheet and bake for 7-10 minutes, or until golden brown.
4. Meanwhile, make frosting by combining ¾ cup powdered sugar, 4 tablespoons butter and 1 ½ teaspoons of orange juice in a small bowl, whisking to combine.
5. Drizzle on or frost warm (not hot) cookies.

**Cookies:**
1 cup sugar
1 cup margarine
1 large egg (two if small or medium)
1 cup cooked pumpkin
2 cups flour
1 teaspoon baking powder
1 teaspoon baking soda
½ cup nuts, pecans or walnuts, chopped (optional)
1 cup dates, chopped (optional)
1 teaspoon vanilla extract

**Frosting:**
¾ cup powdered sugar
4 tablespoons butter
1 ½ teaspoons orange juice

*grandma's pumpkin cookies*

SWEET TREATS AND DESSERTS

# WHITE ROLLED COOKIES *makes 36 cookies*

My mom was known for her decorated cut-out cookies. We baked a double batch of these each year between Thanksgiving and Christmas. Holiday baking took place over multiple days. The day we baked and decorated these cookies was an event in and of itself. I would help by taking them off the cookie tray onto the table and then, when cool, I would spread the base layer of frosting. Then Mom would trim them ever so neatly. My mom has the artistic touch and the steady hand.

---

**1 cup shortening, butter or margarine**
**3 cups flour**
**½ teaspoon baking powder**
**½ teaspoon baking soda**
**2 eggs**
**1 cup sugar, plus additional for the tops of the cookies**

1. In a large bowl, cut shortening into the flour, baking powder and baking soda like a pie crust.
2. In a second bowl using an electric hand mixer, beat eggs and add sugar gradually, continuing to beat thoroughly.
3. Add eggs and sugar to the flour mixture. Knead until smooth.
4. Chill for several hours.
5. Preheat oven to 350°F.
6. Roll the dough until quite thin on a lightly floured board. Cut into cookies.
7. Sprinkle cookies with sugar. Place on a cookie sheet.
8. Bake until creamy in color and crisp, about 8-10 minutes.

# POWDERED SUGAR FROSTING

I don't believe my mom had an actual recipe for powdered sugar frosting for the decorated cookies she would bake for the holidays. It was more of a "put a little sugar in a bowl and add in a little milk until you get the right consistency" kind of recipe. What I do know is that you need to cool them completely or your icing will run.

---

**1 cup powdered sugar**
**2-3 tablespoons milk**
**1 teaspoon vanilla extract**
**food coloring**

1. Gradually add milk until you reach a smooth, easy to spread frosting.
2. Stir in vanilla extract.
3. Once prepared, add food coloring, if desired, stirring the coloring in by spoon.

*Homestyle Desserts*

*Jen having an internal conflict about which pie to choose while Rebecca and Kenny smile for the camera.*

While cookies, cakes and bars were on hand almost all the time on the farm, desserts were reserved for special occasions or a seasonal treat - pies for the holidays, frozen desserts for socials at the church or other special events, pumpkin bread in the fall.

This section features several of the fundamental pie recipes that we frequently baked on the farm along with my favorite dessert recipes from my childhood.

# CRISP - APPLE OR RHUBARB
*serves 12*

This seasonal dessert was made with either apples or rhubarb, during the summer and fall. I personally love it with rhubarb. I prefer desserts that are a little less sweet.

---

**Topping:**
2 cups brown sugar
1 cup butter
2 cups rolled oats
2 cups flour

**Fruit:**
¼ teaspoon nutmeg, or to taste
5 to 6 cups chopped rhubarb or sliced apples
splash or two of lemon juice (for apples only)
pinch or two of salt
½-1 cup sugar
1 teaspoon cinnamon

1. Preheat oven to 350°F.
2. Combine topping ingredients in a bowl. Mix well. Set aside.
3. Generously cover the bottom of a greased 9x13-inch pan with fruit. Add nutmeg, to taste, to fruit.
4. For apples, sprinkle with lemon juice and a pinch or two of salt. Skip the lemon for rhubarb.
5. Add ½ cup sugar (for apples) to 1 cup of sugar (for rhubarb) to the fruit. Sprinkle with cinnamon. Stir gently to combine.
6. Bake until the topping is golden brown and the filling is bubbly, about 45 minutes.

# EASY ROLL PIE CRUST

*2 dough balls for 2 crusts*

This is the pie crust recipe that I have in my collection, handwritten by my mom.

The recipe calls for butter-flavored Crisco for the shortening. Butter-flavored Crisco was introduced in 1981, the year my sister graduated from high school. I was 11 years old.

The debate still rages on in our family as whether butter or shortening is better for pie crusts. Shortening has a high melting point, which aids in creating a tender, flaky crust. Butter, well, nothing tastes better than butter. You can see that the invention of a butter-flavored shortening was a pretty big deal in the world of baking.

---

1. In a medium bowl, mix flour and salt together.
2. Cut in shortening into flour mixture until it turns to coarse crumbs or small peas using a pie blender.
3. Sprinkle with water and blend until all is stuck together well.
4. Place dough in the refrigerator, covered with plastic wrap, for at least 2 hours, up to 24 hours, before rolling.
5. Divide into 2 balls.
6. Flour the countertop, rolling pin and hands.
7. Dust the dough ball and roll out into a circle that is larger than your pie plate, about 12-inch in diameter and about ⅛-inch thick.
8. Use a spatula with a thin edge to pull up the edge of the dough circle, folding in half and then fourths. Place in a pie plate. Unfold the dough and press into the bottom of the pie plate.
9. Repeat for the top crust after filling the pie plate. Place top crust on top of the bottom crust that has been filled with your desired filling. Pinch edges to seal. Slit and decorate top to allow juice and steam to escape.
10. Bake according to the pie filling recipe.

**2 cups flour plus extra for dusting the counter to roll**
**1 teaspoon salt**
**½ cup ice water**
**¾ cup Crisco butter-flavored shortening**

HOMESTYLE DESSERTS

# LEMON MERINGUE PIE

This is my favorite pie, hands down! I find the sweet, tart pudding and the fluffy meringue irresistible. I firmly believe that there is always room for lemon meringue pie. It is just a lovely ending after a rich and hearty farmhouse meal.

My dad, now in his 80s, has always been quite the pie baker. Baking a lemon meringue pie is a labor of love - slowly simmering the pudding, made from freshly squeezed lemons, on the stove. It is always such a special treat when he makes it, and even more special was when we made it together.

---

**1 pre-baked pie crust (Page 171)**

**Lemon Filling:**
**1 cup sugar**
**1 ¼ cups water**
**1 tablespoon butter**
**¼ cup cornstarch mixed with 3 tablespoons of cold water**
**6 tablespoons fresh lemon juice**
**1 teaspoon lemon zest**
**2 tablespoons cornstarch**
**3 large egg yolks**
**2 tablespoons milk**

1. Preheat oven to 350°F.
2. Combine sugar, 1 ¼ cups water and butter in a Dutch oven; heat until sugar dissolves. Add cornstarch that has been combined with cold water. Stir to combine.
3. Cook slowly until thick and bubbly, stirring constantly.
4. Add lemon juice and zest; cook for 2 minutes.

## MERINGUE

1. Combine ingredients and beat on high with an electric handheld mixer.
2. Beat until stiff peaks form.
3. Spread on top of a lemon, banana or other custard pie and bake according to pie recipe directions.

**3 egg whites**
**6 tablespoons sugar**
**1 teaspoon lemon juice**

# BANANA CREAM PIE

Lemon meringue pie is my favorite, but this banana pie is its rival. If Dad had a little more time on his hands, he liked to bake banana cream pie. Made-from-scratch vanilla pudding sets this apart from other banana cream pies.

When Mom or Dad contributed a pie to a bake sale or church supper, they always sold fast. I don't remember bringing home anything other than an empty pan.

The recipe for meringue can be found with the lemon pie recipe in this section.

---

1. Preheat oven to 350°F.
2. Stir together sugar, cornstarch and salt.
3. In a Dutch oven, add sugar mixture, milk and eggs. Cook over medium heat until it boils. Cook 1 minute longer. Add butter and vanilla.
4. Slice bananas over a baked pie shell. Add pudding and top with meringue.
5. Bake at 350°F until meringue is golden brown, about 10-12 minutes. Watch closely to prevent the peaks from burning.

1 pre-baked pie crust (Page 171)

**Banana Filling:**
⅔ cup sugar
¼ cup plus cornstarch
½ teaspoon salt
3 cups milk
4 egg yolks, slightly beaten
2 tablespoons butter
1 tablespoon plus 1 teaspoon vanilla
2 large bananas

**Meringue (Page 171)**

*banana cream pie*

HOMESTYLE DESSERTS

# PUMPKIN PIE

Thanksgiving with our family was not complete without pumpkin pie. I am not sure I have had better pumpkin pie than this family recipe. Somehow there was always room for a small slice, even after a Thanksgiving feast. The biggest questions were how you wanted it served; warm or cold or with whipped topping or naked.

---

2 large eggs, slightly beaten
16 ounces cooked pumpkin or squash
¾ cup sugar
½ teaspoon salt
1 teaspoon cinnamon
½ teaspoon ginger
¼ teaspoon cloves
1 ⅔ cups evaporated milk or light cream
1 9-inch pie shell (Page 171)

1. Preheat oven to 425°F.
2. In a large bowl, mix ingredients in the order listed. Pour into the pie shell.
3. Bake for 15 minutes.
4. Reduce heat to 350°F. Continue baking for about 40 minutes or until a knife inserted in the center comes out clean.

# BLUEBERRY PIE

Another pie that my dad enjoys baking (and eating) is blueberry. You can always find blueberries fresh or frozen, no matter the time of year. Frozen blueberries were kept in our freezer on the farm year-round, ready for any occasion that called for a pie. I would not be surprised if there were blueberries in the freezer at Mom and Dad's lake home on Ottertail Lake right now.

---

1. Preheat oven to 350°F.
2. In a bowl, mix blueberries, sugar, lemon juice and four.
3. In a pie plate lined with the unbaked pie crust, add blueberries mixture. Dot with butter and a pinch or so of nutmeg.
4. Layer on top crust. Trim the excess from the top crust. Crimp edges. Vent crust with a sharp knife.
5. Bake for 40 minutes then turn down to 325°F for 15 minutes.

**3 cups blueberries**
**¾ cup sugar**
**3 tablespoons lemon juice**
**4 tablespoons flour (scant)**
**1 tablespoon butter, cold, cut into small cubes**
**pinch or two of nutmeg**
**2 (top and bottom) pie crusts (Page 171)**

*Tidbits from Jen's Kitchen*

Venting and crimping the top crust allow the pie to release steam, preventing a soggy crust while keeping the filling inside. They also give your pie personality. Mom's preferred crimping style was the scalloped crimp. To scallop your crust, use your index finger to push down on the edge of the dough and then use the finger and thumb of your other hand to pinch the dough either side. Repeat around the rim of the pie. The end result looks like the edge of the gorgeous piece of pie in Megan's photograph once baked.

The simplest way to add vents to the top of your pie crust is to simply cut slits in the top with a sharp knife. Mom was known for her beautiful butterflies on the tops of hers but you don't need to get that elaborate. Five 2-inch slits, arranged in a circle radiating from the center and pointing out to the edge like a star is a simple and beautiful way to vent your crust.

# SHORTCAKE *serves 8*

Summer on the farm in Minnesota meant seasonal fruit. There was no better way to feature the summer fruits than over a fresh, warm piece of shortcake and a generous dollop of fresh whipped cream. Strawberries or peaches over shortcake represent summer to me. This shortcake comes together quickly and is so light and flaky.

---

**2 cups flour**
**2 teaspoons baking powder**
**¾ teaspoon salt**
**3 tablespoons sugar**
**⅔ cup vegetable oil**
**¾ cup milk**
**fresh berries or peaches**
**fresh whipped cream or ice cream**

1. Preheat oven to 425°F.
2. Add all dry ingredients and stir well. Add oil and milk all at once. Blend only until combined. Some lumps will remain. Do not over mix.
3. Bake in an 8x8-inch greased glass baking dish.
4. To serve, cut in 2-inch squares. Slice in half, place half on the bottom of a bowl and top with fresh berries or peaches and whipped cream. Place the other half on top. Repeat with more berries and whipped topping, if desired. Best when served hot.

# PEACHES *serves 4*

Mom would buy crates of fresh peaches for canning each year. I looked forward to peach season. I am honestly more of a fan of fresh than canned. (Please don't tell anyone else in our family my secret. It might cause controversy.)

This simple peach sauce is delicious over shortcake, angel food cake (Page 148) or ice cream. The addition of rum butter is my secret to an extra special peach dessert.

---

**4 ripe peaches**
**2 teaspoons sugar**
**3 tablespoons butter, unsalted, melted**
**3 tablespoons dark rum**

1. To quickly peel peaches, cut a small "X" on the bottom of each. Slip peaches into a large pot of boiling water.
2. Boil for about 30 seconds, then remove with a slotted spoon and submerge immediately in a bowl of ice water to stop the cooking. Slip off the skins with your fingers.
3. Run a sharp knife vertically around the outside of the peach starting with the stem end. Twist the peach carefully to pull it apart into two and remove the pit. Slice each half into ¼-inch slices or dice peaches into ¼-inch pieces.
4. In a small bowl, combine the sliced peaches and 2 teaspoons granulated sugar. Set aside.
5. In another small bowl, combine rum and butter. Whisk to combine.
6. Serve peaches over shortcake or ice cream, drizzled with rum butter.

# STRAWBERRY YOGURT DESSERT

*serves 8*

This recipe reminds me of summertime church social gatherings growing up. No better way to finish a ladies' luncheon in the summer than with an "ice box" dessert made with Cool Whip and fresh fruit. This dessert, with its homemade graham cracker crust, was such a treat on a hot summer day.

Cool Whip was first introduced in 1966. Cool Whip became a quintessential Minnesota dessert ingredient in the years to follow. Would you be surprised to find out that was invented by a Minnesota-born chemist? William H. Mitchell was a chemist for General Foods who is also credited for the creation of quick-set Jell-O, Tang and Cool Whip.

Cool Whip provided a convenient way to have a whipped topping at a moment's notice. Cool Whip quickly became a staple on the farm as we always had room for a container or two in the large chest freezer in the farmhouse basement.

---

1. Preheat oven to 425°F.
2. Mix crust ingredients in a medium bowl and then press into a 9x13-inch pan. Bake for 16-17 minutes.
3. Combine the filling ingredients in a bowl and mix. Set aside or refrigerate.
4. Let the graham cracker crust cool and then crumble. Reserve ⅓ of the mixture for topping.
5. Press ⅔ of the crust mixture into a pie plate. Top with filling. Then sprinkle the remaining crumbled crust on top.
6. Freeze until firm, at least 4 hours or overnight.

**Crust:**
½ cup brown sugar
1 cup margarine
2 cups flour
1 cup pecans or walnuts, finely chopped

**Strawberry Yogurt Filling:**
2 8-ounce containers strawberry yogurt (or another flavor that pairs with your choice of fruit)
1 8-ounce package frozen Cool Whip whipped topping
½ cup mashed strawberries (or fruit of your choice)

HOMESTYLE DESSERTS

# BANANA SPLIT FROZEN DESSERT

*serves 24*

Frozen desserts like this one were not made frequently. Instead, they were reserved for special occasions in the summer months or for church functions where you need to serve a large group. It is essentially a banana split in dessert form. It is a wonderful dessert to serve on a hot summer day. It's also a make-ahead recipe so if you plan ahead, all you have to do is grab it out of the freezer and serve!

---

**Crust:**
3 ⅓ cups graham cracker crumbs
6 tablespoons plus 2 teaspoons sugar
⅔ cup plus 2 tablespoons butter, melted

**Banana Layer:**
3 bananas
lemon juice, to prevent browning, if desired
chopped nuts (peanuts, pecans, walnuts)

**Ice Cream Layer:**
vanilla ice cream, softened

**Chocolate Layer:**
6 ounces milk chocolate chips
½ cup butter
2 cups powdered sugar
1 ½ cups evaporated milk
1 teaspoon vanilla extract

**Top Layer:**
2 cups whipped cream
pinch or two sugar

1. Mix graham cracker crumbs with sugar and butter. Pat into the bottom of a 9x13-inch pan, reserving 1 cup for the top.
2. Slice 3 bananas into thin coins. Toss in lemon juice to prevent browning, if desired. Layer bananas over the crust.
3. Place ice cream in a ½-inch layer over the bananas and sprinkle with nuts. Freeze.
4. Melt the chocolate chips in a saucepan with butter, powdered sugar and milk. Cook over low heat until very thick and smooth. Stir continuously. Remove from heat and stir in vanilla. Cool. Then pour over frozen ice cream.
5. Freeze until firm.
6. Whip 2 cups of whipping cream until very stiff. Add a pinch or two of sugar (to taste) and combine. Pour over the chocolate layer. Sprinkle with reserved graham cracker crumbs. Freeze until ready to serve.
7. Remove from the freezer 10-15 minutes before serving.

HOMESTYLE DESSERTS

# MAPLE WALNUT ICE CREAM
*makes 1 qt*

  Ice cream by the pail was always in the chest freezer at the farm. You would find at least one pail of New York vanilla and perhaps another flavor like butter pecan or maple walnut in the freezer at any time. Ice cream was served as dessert all on its own or as a topping for pies, crisps or brownies.

  Although we did not make our own ice cream on the farm as a child, we have since acquired an ice cream maker for Mom and Dad for their lake home on Ottertail Lake. Knowing Dad's love of this nutty ice cream, this was the recipe we first made together at the lake. It has been adapted from the original recipe featured in "Perfect Scoop" by David Lebovitz.

  Rumor has it that Mom was caught sneaking tastes from the freezer to protect her share the first time we churned up a batch. It has become a fun new tradition, based on old memories, to make ice cream on our visits.

  I prefer to make ice cream the day before I plan to serve it. Freeze in a plastic container overnight so that it has a chance to firm up before serving.

---

**1 ½ cups whole milk**
**2 tablespoons sugar**
**1 ½ cups heavy cream**
**5 large eggs yolks**
**¾ cup maple syrup**
**pinch of sea salt**
**½ teaspoon vanilla extract**
**Wet Walnuts (recipe follows)**

1. Warm the milk and sugar in a saucepan until the sugar is dissolved. Stirring constantly.
2. Pour the heavy cream into a medium bowl and set a fine mesh strainer on top.
3. In another medium bowl, whisk the egg yolks. Slowly pour the warm mixture into the egg yolks, a little at a time. Whisk constantly. Add the warmed egg yolk mixture back into the saucepan.
4. Stir the egg mixture constantly over medium heat with a spatula or wooden spoon, ensuring the mixture does not stick to the bottom or scorch. Custard is done when it thickens and coats the back of the spatula.
5. Pour the custard through the fine mesh strainer into the cool cream. Add the maple syrup, salt, and vanilla.
6. Place over a large bowl filled with ice. Stir custard until cool.
7. Chill the mixture in the refrigerator.
8. Freeze it in your ice cream maker, as instructed. During the last few minutes of churning, add the Wet Walnuts.

# WET WALNUTS

1. Heat the maple syrup in a small saucepan until it just begins to come to a boil.
2. Stir in the walnuts, then cook until it returns to a boil once again.
3. Remove them from the heat immediately and let cool completely. The nuts will still be wet and sticky when cooled.

**⅓ cup maple syrup**
**1 ½ cups walnuts, finely chopped**
**a pinch of sea salt**

# GRANDMA MCKEE'S LEMON BREAD
*serves 12*

My mom loves to bake this recipe from her mother, Phyllis McKee. It tasted like fresh lemons to me, and was so moist and tender. It's a sweet bread you can serve for brunch or as a dessert.

Mom bakes this bread to this day. She made a gluten-free version with almond flour for my friend, Nancy O'Dell, when she and I visited my parents at their winter home in Mesa, Arizona. It turned out delightful. The bread was so delicious that Nancy had to have a copy of the recipe before we left to explore Sedona and the Grand Canyon.

---

1. Preheat oven to 325°F.
2. In a large bowl, blend butter and 1 cup of sugar. Beat in egg one at a time.
3. In a small bowl, combine flour, baking powder, and salt, stirring to combine.
4. Then add dry ingredients to the butter and sugar, alternating with milk mixture.
5. Fold in lemon peel and nuts.
6. Pour in a greased loaf pan. Bake for 60-75 minutes.
7. Mix lemon juice and ½ cup of sugar together and spoon over the hot loaf.
8. Cool for 10 minutes and remove from the loaf pan.

**⅓ cup melted butter**
**1 cup sugar**
**2 eggs**
**1 ½ cups flour**
**1 teaspoon baking powder**
**½ teaspoon salt**
**¼ teaspoon almond extract (add to milk)**
**½ cup milk**
**1 tablespoon grated lemon peels**
**½ cup chopped nuts**
**3 tablespoons fresh lemon juice**
**½ cup sugar**

HOMESTYLE DESSERTS

**Megan's Recipe Secret:**

Substitute a little protein powder instead of flour for an added protein boost!

# BANANA BREAD

*serves 8*

This is another recipe that I have been baking since I was a little girl. We had banana bread quite frequently. Everyone liked it and it was a great way to use up those overripe bananas.

Our family recipe is moist and dense, with an almost pound-cake-like texture. It is loaded with bananas and has just a touch of buttermilk. These are the recipe secrets, setting it apart from other banana bread recipes I have experimented with over the years.

---

1. Preheat oven to 350°F.
2. In a large bowl, cream butter with sugar. Add eggs and bananas and mix well.
3. In a small bowl, mix baking soda into flour.
4. Stir in buttermilk and flour mixture into banana mixture and stir until combined.
5. Pour into a greased loaf pan.
6. Bake for 1 hour or until a toothpick inserted into the middle comes out clean.

**½ cup butter or shortening**
**1 cup sugar**
**2 large eggs**
**4 bananas, mashed**
**1 ½ tablespoons buttermilk**
**2 cups flour**
**1 teaspoon baking soda (mixed into flour)**
**1 cup pecans or walnuts, chopped**

*banana bread*

# PUMPKIN BREAD

*serves 8*

I admit I am partial to baking sweet breads. They are great for breakfast as well as for dessert. This is my go-to recipe for pumpkin bread. Super moist and dense, it is almost like pumpkin pound cake.

This recipe was in the Vukku Centennial Cookbook, first published in 1990 as part of the church's centennial celebration. My mom gave me a copy while I was in college. It was my very first cookbook. It is a treasure as it contains many recipes our family enjoyed at our church's potlucks and celebrations. This recipe was submitted by Shirley Brause, one of the members.

Vukku Lutheran was our country church located just a few miles from the farm. Our Norwegian ancestors were founding members when it was established in 1890. The church was named after their home church in Verdal, Norway.

I attended Sunday school and made my first friends at Vukku. I was confirmed and then taught Sunday school myself before graduating from high school and heading off to college. I have fond memories of the members of this church. Attending Sunday school and participating in its youth group were the foundation for many wonderful friendships, some lifelong.

---

1. Preheat oven to 350°F.
2. Combine sugar, oil and eggs in a stand mixer. Cream. Add pumpkin and water, mix to combine.
3. In a medium bowl, add spices, baking soda and ½ cup flour, mix to combine.
4. Add the flour mixture to the wet ingredients in the mixer's bowl and stir to combine. Add remaining flour and stir until just combined.
5. Place batter into greased pans: two 9x5-inch or four 5x2-inch.
6. Bake for 1 hour, or until a toothpick inserted in the middle comes clean.
7. Cool for 10 minutes, then turn out of the pan and finish cooling on a rack.

**3 cups sugar**
**1 cup vegetable oil**
**4 eggs**
**⅔ cup water**
**1 ½ cups pumpkin**
**2 teaspoons baking soda**
**3 ½ cups flour**
**1-2 teaspoons cinnamon**
**1 teaspoon nutmeg**
**½ cup walnuts (optional)**

**Megan's Recipe Secret:**

Semi-sweet chocolate chips work well with this recipe in place of milk chocolate.

# AUNT KARYN'S TURTLES

This is my mom's sister, Karyn Kyte's, recipe for turtles. Karyn is my mom's only sibling. She moved out of state with her family when I was little. Sadly, we did not often have a chance to see her and her family since they were an plane flight away. What I do remember as a young child is getting a box each Christmas filled with homemade sweet treats and goodies. The box would include turtles and her fudge along with other holiday candies and cookies. We all waited with anticipation for its arrival! Turtles were also one of my dad's favorite candies. I mean, how could you not love anything that was a combination of crunchy nuts, gooey caramels and creamy milk chocolate? Yum! Needless to stay, there was often a bit of a fight over these turtles when they arrived.

---

1. In a double boiler, melt caramels and butter together. Add 2 cups of pecans.
2. Spoon onto a greased cookie sheet or waxed paper. Let cool completely.
3. Stick toothpicks into the caramel layer.
4. In a double boiler, melt chocolate and paraffin together.
5. Using the toothpick, dip caramels into chocolate. Place on cookie sheet. Alternatively, pour a ½ spoonful of chocolate over the caramel layer.
6. Let cool.

**1 package of caramels, unwrapped**
**1 stick of butter**
**12 ounces of milk chocolate chips**
**1 ounce paraffin wax**
**2 cups of pecan halves**

# Preserving it: Canning & Freezing

*Jenny picking plums on the farm.*

Canning and freezing produce was just part of farm life. It was not summer or fall without canning peaches, pears, pickles and plum juice or freezing corn and green beans.

Over the years, preserving foods through canning and freezing has sadly fallen out of favor as our busy lives and modern-day conveniences have taken its place.

Megan's love of gardening has rekindled this family tradition. I enjoy talking with her and my parents about it and helping carry on this heritage.

I hope this collection of basic instructions and recipes that I grew up with inspires you to give preserving fresh produce a try. I guarantee you once you have mastered the basics, the results of your labor will be well worth the effort.

# CANNING- THE BASICS

Canning is a method to preserve food in jars at high temperatures for a long period of time. Canning kills microorganisms and inactivates enzymes that cause food to spoil. The heating process pushes air from the jar and then creates a vacuum seal as food cools. There are two methods: water bath canning and pressure canning. We used the water bath method on the farm.

Water bath canning is a lower temperature canning process. It is perfect for high-acid foods and recipes that incorporate the proper amount of acid. It is recommended for fruits, jams, jellies, salsa, tomatoes, pickles, chutneys, sauces, pie fillings, and condiments.

Our Minnesota farm was 20 miles from the nearest town with a grocery store. Canning was an essential farm activity because it stocked the pantry for the long winter. Beyond that, the results really are superior to anything you can buy in the store. I think Megan and my nephews, Matthew, Michael, and David Bissinger would support me in that statement.

Each summer we canned peaches, pears, cherries and pickles. In addition, Mom would often preserve tomato sauce along with plum and grape juice for making jelly. Canning day was a hands-on, all-day event.

Megan has rekindled the family canning tradition. She started canning a few years ago to ensure the bounty from their garden would not go to waste. Watching her preserve produce like her grandparents makes my heart happy as she carries on this tradition.

Nowadays, people have become intimidated by canning, believing you must make huge batches in order to preserve fresh produce. Canning is more approachable than you may think. The superior product is worth the labor of love. This section provides the basics of canning. My hope is that by sharing this family tradition of food preservation, it will inspire you to try small batch canning to capture the best flavors of the summer and fall.

# TIPS AND TRICKS

You should always use fresh produce and can your fruits and vegetables when they are at their peak.

Do not use any bruised or overripe produce.

Don't overfill your jars. Follow the instructions from your recipe for headspace. Headspace is the amount of room from the food in the jar to the top of the jar. Overfilling can result in jars that don't seal properly.

An unsealed jar does not mean the world has come to an end. You can refrigerate the jar and use the jar within the next few days or reprocess. When reprocessing, return the jar to room temperature before re-processing and ensure you have sufficient headspace.

Unopened and properly sealed canned produce has a shelf life of up to one year while jams and jellies made using sugar and processed in a hot water bath can last up to two years.

While most canned produce is shelf-stable, it can go bad. You can tell if a jar has gone bad by looking for a bulging lid, rust on the lid, bubbles when you open the jar, mold or cloudy contents or the contents has an odor when you open the jar.

Canning Equipment:
- canning tongs for lifting jars
- ladle
- wide-mouth funnel
- canning jars and seals
- large pot or water-bath canner
- wooden skewer or butter knife
- kitchen towels

# WATER BATH CANNING STEPS

Step 1. Wash canning jars in hot, soapy water. Rinse well. Place jars in a water bath canner or other deep, large pot. Cover with hot water and simmer over medium heat. Keep them in hot simmering water until they are ready to fill. Place lids in a bowl and pour hot water from your pot over top of the lids.

Step 2. Using your canning tongs, remove a jar from the hot water bath and place on a kitchen towel. Place funnel atop the jar and ladle produce into the jar. Leave ¼-½-inch of headspace at the top.

Step 3. Release any trapped air bubbles by gently stirring contents with a long wooden skewer or a butter knife, being careful not to damage the produce.

Step 4. Wipe rims of jars dry and screw on lids.

Step 5. Using your canning tongs, place each filled jar gently in the canner. Be sure that the jars do not touch each other.

Step 6. When all the jars have been placed inside, cover by 1 inch of water.

Step 7. Cover the canner and heat the water to a rolling boil.

Step 8. Boil jars as recommended by your recipe, generally around 10 minutes. Remove jars with your tongs and place on the towel on the counter.

Step 9. Let them cool to room temperature. You will hear the jars ping shortly after they have been removed from the canner. If you do not hear this sound, they have not properly sealed. The center of properly sealed jars will have a concave center of the lid from the vacuum (airtight) seal.

Step 10. Test seals by pressing the center of jar lids once they have cooled completely. If the lid is not firm and tight and moves up and down, then the jar has not sealed. Place any unsealed jars in the refrigerator for immediate use or re- process the following day.

# CANNING PEACHES (AND OTHER FRUIT)

Canning season on the farm was late summer. We would preserve peaches, pears and cherries for the long Minnesota winter. Of course, we also canned pickles. Pears were my favorite canned fruit. Peaches, however, were the most-loved by others in our family including Megan and my nephew, Michael Bissinger.

Mom would pick up crates of peaches to process each summer. As they ripened on the table in the basement, nestled under newspaper, she would pluck the ripe ones to use immediately. The rest would be used for canning. Processing each fruit was a full-day affair. It was well worth it as we had fruit to enjoy all winter. Home-canned fruit is nothing like that from the store.

You can vary the amount of sugar and water based on the tartness of the fruit and adjust the sweetness to the level that you desire. You can also use honey instead of sugar.

Mom's preference was a light syrup for pears and a medium syrup for peaches and cherries. The ratios below are from The All New Ball Book of Canning and Preserving, which is still the canning and preserving bible for our family.

| Syrup | Ratio | Yield |
| --- | --- | --- |
| Extra Light | 1 ¼ cups sugar to 5 ½ cups water | Yields 6 cups |
| Light | 2 ¼ cups sugar to 5 ½ cups | Yields 7 cups |
| Medium | 3 ¼ cups sugar to 5 cups water | Yields 7 cups |
| Heavy | 4 ¼ cups sugar to 4 ¼ cups water | Yields 7 cups |
| Honey | 1 cup liquid honey to 4 cups water | Yields 5 cups |

CANNING AND FREEZING

**peaches**
**water**
**sugar or honey**
**lemon juice or citric acid**

1. Prepare the water bath canner by filling it with water. Add enough water to cover the jars by 2 inches once the water is boiling.
2. Set the canner on the stove. Turn the burner to high. Once it reaches a boil, reduce it to simmer. Keep the water hot so that everything is ready when the peaches are.
3. Wash and sanitize your jars. Keep the jars warm to avoid having them crack when placed in the canner.
4. Wash the lids and set aside in a clean place or keep in a small saucepan simmering in water.
5. Add one layer of peaches at a time to a pot of boiling water for about 1 minute. Remove when the skin starts to come away from the flesh. Remove using a slotted spoon and place in an ice bath for 1 minute.
6. Use the slotted spoon to remove the peaches from the ice bath. Grab one of the peaches and gently peel the skin back.
7. Use a paring knife and cut the peach around the middle to separate. Remove the pit. Put the halves in a large bowl of water treated with citric acid.
8. In a medium-sized pot, combine sugar and water to create the syrup.
9. Add the peaches to the warm canning jars with a fork or spoon. Repeat with other peach halves until the jar is filled. Depending on the size of the peaches, each quart will fit about 3-4 peaches.
10. At this point, return the water in the canner back to a rolling boil.
11. Using a canning funnel, ladle hot syrup into the jars, leaving ½-inch of headspace. (Headspace is the distance between the top of the food and the top of the jar.) Use a spoon to pack down the peaches a bit, if necessary.
12. Using a long utensil such as a wooden spoon, remove all the air bubbles by running it gently around the inside edges of the jar.
13. Clean the rim of the jar very well with a warm damp rag. Place a lid on the jar. Add a ring and tighten.
14. Gently place the jars in the canner. Put the lid on and set a timer. Pints should process for 20 minutes, and quarts for 25 minutes.
15. Once the peaches have processed for the appropriate amount of time, remove the canner from the burner, remove the lid, and allow it to sit for 5-10 minutes.
16. Carefully remove the jars and place them on a thick towel in a place where they can be undisturbed for 12 hours. The lids should start to pop within 20-30 minutes of being removed from the water. That popping sound is essential as it tells you that everything is sealed.
17. After the jars have rested for about 12 hours, press down in the middle of each lid. The lid should not give at all. If it does, it did not seal. Any unseal jars can be refrigerated and used that same week.
18. Canned peaches will last for 9-12 months.

# PICKLES WITH DILL AND GARLIC

*makes 7 quart jars*

Pickles. One of the major canning events of the summer season on the farm. I have always been a huge fan of pickles, possibly a fanatic. This recipe is our family recipe for basic garlic dill pickles. I could devour the whole jar if left unattended as a child.

Megan has always loved pickles too. She gets that from me, I suspect. She has been canning her own for some time now, feeding her craving for her grandparents' garlic dill pickles. She is a little more adventurous than her grandparents in her canning efforts. She is now canning other vegetables and adds jalapeños and other peppers to her pickles for a kick.

---

1. To each jar, add one 1 clove garlic, sliced and a sprig of dill. Divide washed and cleaned cucumbers between the jars, packing them as tightly as possible.
2. In a medium size pot, combine water, vinegar, sugar, pickling salt and alum, if using. Heat over medium-high heat until the mixture boils and sugar and salt have dissolved.
3. Pour hot mixture into prepared jars, leaving 1-½ inches of headspace. Place on lids and tighten firmly but do not over tighten.
4. Put jars into a cold water bath. Process for 3 minutes to kill any bacteria. Bring to a boil then turn down to medium-low and simmer for 3 minutes.
5. Remove after 3 minutes and stand upright. Let cool.

**pickling cucumbers (small, evenly sized), washed and cleaned**
**1 bud garlic, for each jar, peeled and sliced**
**fresh dill sprigs**
**11 cups water**
**2 cups vinegar**
**⅔ cup sugar**
**1 cup pickling salt**
**¼ teaspoon alum (optional)**

CANNING AND FREEZING

# MAKING JELLY - THE BASICS

Some families are jam families; some are jelly fans. We were a jelly family. Homemade jelly was a staple on the farm. Canning jelly, like canning fruits, is more approachable than you may think. We have included some basics to get you started.

Jelly is made from extracted fruit juice instead of whole fruit. It is then cooked with sugar and pectin to thicken to a firm but spreadable consistency. Its flavor is richer and deeper than store-bought alternatives. Fruits like tart apples, crab apples, cranberries, blackberries, wild plums, concord grapes and currants are perfect for jelly as they have a high pectin content. You will want to use firm ripe fruit for the best results.

Sugar, when combined with the pectin and fruit acids, allow the fruit to gel. If you use too little sugar, you will know because your jelly will not set. Don't be too disappointed, instead of jelly, you have created a wonderful syrup for pancakes or a sauce for ice cream. We had this happen from time to time on the farm. On the other hand, if your jelly is really stiff and not spreadable, then you have used too much sugar. The secret is in finding the right amount of sugar, and each batch of fruit can vary from year to year.

Pectin creates the gelling effect. Fruit contains pectin naturally but not all fruit has enough to gel on its own. Adding pectin or a high pectin ingredient like lemon juice ensures your fruit will gel. For the most part, we followed the instructions on the pectin box growing up. This is our adapted family version of that old box recipe.

Equipment

- large pot or saucepan
- jelly jars and lids
- wooden spoon
- cheesecloth (optional)
- water-bath canner
- kitchen towels

# STEPS TO MAKE JELLY

Step 1. Sterilize jars and lids by simmering in boiling water for 10 minutes or more.
Step 2. Prepare fruit as directed by the package instructions included with your pectin.
Step 3. Place several layers of damp cheesecloth in a large bowl. Pour fruit into cheesecloth. Tie cheesecloth closed. Hang and let drip into a bowl until the dripping stops. Then press gently to extract as much juice as possible.
Step 4. Use a measuring cup to measure the amount of prepared juice into your pot. If necessary, add water to get the quantity needed for your recipe. Don't add more than ½ cup of water.
Step 5. Add lemon juice or water as instructed by directions on the pectin package.
Step 6. Add sugar. The amount of sugar will be based on the fruit.
Step 7. Prepare jelly according to pectin package directions.
Step 8. Ladle jelly into prepared jars, leaving ¼-inch of headroom at the top.
Step 9. Wipe the rim of the jar dry. Cover with seal and ring.
Step 10. Place jars on the elevated rack in the canner and lower rack into the canner. Water must cover jars by a least 1 inch, up to 2 inches. Add more boiling water, if needed.
Step 11. Cover; bring water to a gentle boil. Process 5 minutes or as noted on the pectin package.
Step 12. Remove jars and place on a towel to cool completely.
Step 13. After jars cool, check seals by pressing the centers of lids with your fingers. If the lid is not firm and gives, the lid is not sealed. Refrigerate for immediate use (up to three weeks).
Step 14. Let prepared jars stand at room temperature 24 hours, or until set.
Step 15. Store unopened jellies in a cool, dry, dark place for up to 1 year. Refrigerate opened jellies for up to 3 weeks.

# MAKING FREEZER JELLY

You can also freeze jelly, which is even easier. Follow instructions above but instead of moving to the canning phase, place jelly in freezer-proof containers, leaving ½-inch of headroom. Cover with lids.

Let stand at room temperature 24 hours or until set.

Refrigerate up to 3 weeks or freeze for up to 1 year. If frozen, thaw in the refrigerator before using.

# WILD PLUM JAM

*8 half-pint jars*

Is there anything better than plum and grape jelly on top of homemade fresh baked and buttered bread? It was a wonderfully delicious way to start the day. I believe this could be one of Megan's most cherished food memories from visits to the farm or the lake. You'll have to ask her to be sure. I also would put money on it ranking pretty high in my nephews' - Matthew, Michael and David Bissinger - fondest food memories too.

We would use the juice from plum groves on the farm. Wild plums are more tart and smaller than their tame, cultivated counterparts. If you don't have access to wild plums, you will want to decrease the amount of sugar in the recipe. The All New Ball Big Book of Canning and Preserving recommends 1 cup of sugar per 1 pound of ripe plums.

Some years were lucky enough to be gifted wild grapes from a neighbor or family. Since wild grapes are hard to come by these days, you can use Concord or Scuppernong grapes in their place. You will need less water for grape jelly, reducing it to 1 cup of water for 6 pounds of grapes and decreasing the sugar to 7 cups of sugar.

---

1. In a stockpot, simmer plums and water until tender, about 30 minutes. Line a fine mesh strainer with four layers of cheesecloth and place over a bowl. Place plum mixture in a strainer then cover with edges of cheesecloth. Let stand for 30 minutes or until the liquid measures 5 ½ cups.
2. Return liquid to the stockpot. Add pectin; stir and bring to a boil. Add sugar; bring to a full rolling boil. Boil for 1 minute, stirring constantly.
3. Remove from the heat and skim off any foam. Carefully ladle the hot mixture into hot sterilized half-pint jars, leaving ½-inch of headspace. Remove air bubbles; wipe rims and adjust lids.
4. Process for 5 minutes in a boiling-water canner. Carefully remove jars from the canner and follow the basic canning steps above to cool and check the jars.

**5 pounds wild plums, halved and pitted**
**4 cups water**
**1 package (1 ¾ ounces) powdered pectin**
**7 ½ cups sugar**

# APPLE BUTTER

As much as I love Dad's jelly, apple butter also ranked high on my list of preferred toppings for toast or a slice of fresh baked bread. It is easy to make and fills the whole house with the fragrances of fall.

Apple pulp is apples that have been chopped, cooked and run through a food mill. To make apple pulp, cut the apples into quarters. Do not core or peel them. Place them in a large pot with apple cider. Bring to a rolling boil, stirring often so the apples do not stick to the bottom of the pot. Cover and reduce heat, simmering the apple mixture until the apples are soft, about 30 minutes.

Run batches of cooked apples through a food mill into a large bowl. The mill will separate the peelings and seeds, leaving a thick apple pulp. Continue milling the apples until all have been reduced to pulp. Discard the peelings and seeds.

---

1. Add all ingredients to a large pot or Dutch oven including the lemon rind.
2. Bring to a boil and boil until thick. Stir frequently to prevent sticking to the bottom of the pot.
3. Remove lemon rind. Let cool.
4. Cool; apple butter will thicken as it cools.

**8 cups apples pulp (2 quarts)**
**6 cups sugar**
**2-3 tablespoons cinnamon**
**1 teaspoon nutmeg**
**1 teaspoons salt**
**juice of one lemon, rind cut into pieces**

*Tidbits from Jen's Kitchen*
I prefer to freeze apple butter. Once it is cool, I ladle it into the freezer containers, leaving ½-inch of space at the top. Seal the containers and place in the freezer. It will freeze well for up to a year. You can keep it in the refrigerator for about 3 weeks to a month, once thawed and opened.

# FREEZING – THE BASICS

Mom and Dad have had a big chest freezer for as long as I can remember. When I was a child, the freezer stored a side of beef, a whole pig and chickens purchased each year from neighboring farms. It was quite a shock for me to buy meat in the grocery store for the first time when I was in college. I was underwhelmed. The quality of meat we had growing up was amazing. You can still find farmers that are willing to sell to you directly or you can buy through a community-supported agriculture (CSA). I try to go this route whenever I can, and highly recommend it.

The freezer was also chock full of frozen vegetables for the long winter months. We froze green beans, corn and squash from our garden each year. Frozen blueberries, strawberries and peaches were often found in our farm freezer too. Berries are great to freeze and require very little effort - strawberries, raspberries, blackberries or blueberries. Just lay flat on a tray, freeze then when frozen solid toss in a freezer bag. Done!

Frozen vegetables taste so much better than canned. If you want to enjoy your fresh vegetables even after the summer ends, just follow the simple steps below. While we have included the basic information on freezing vegetables to get your started, I suggest you pick up a book on preserving and canning if you are interested in learning more on how to stock your freezer like we did on the farm.

Many vegetables require blanching in boiling water before freezing, as described below. Blanching destroys the enzymes that keep the ripening process moving forward. Blanching also aids in removing any remaining dirt or bacteria without destroying the nutrients and brightens the color of the vegetables. Use one gallon of water for each pound of vegetables.

If you are going to freeze squash, you will not blanch it as described below. Instead, cook or roast until tender then cool. Once cooled you can move directly to the packing in a freezer bag or container.

## STEPS FOR FREEZING VEGETABLES

Step 1. Prepare the produce by cutting into chunks or slices and remove any stems, as needed.
Step 2. Cook them in boiling water for one to three minutes.
Step 3. Immediately remove from water and place the vegetables in a bowl of ice water. Cool completely.
Step 4. Drain the water and pat the vegetables dry.
Step 5. Place on a baking sheet, making a single layer of vegetables and freeze them until solid.
Step 6. Once frozen, pack them into freezer bags or containers designed for freezing. Alternatively, you can skip freezing on a baking sheet and place directly into freezer-safe containers.
Step 7. Squeeze out any excess air and seal the bag or container.

**Megan's Recipe Secret:**

For something more savory, omit the sugar and add bell peppers. I use dehydrated green peppers!

# CREAMED SWEET CORN
*makes 4 quarts*

Minnesota sweet corn from the Red River Valley is still the best I have ever had, hands down. I suspect it is the rich soil in the valley that makes the corn grown in our farming community so delightful. My sister, Rebecca, and I still talk about how we have not been able to find corn remotely as good anywhere else.

Uncle Reynold would plant a large garden each summer on their family farm, which was "just down the road a piece" from ours. He loved his garden. Corn, potatoes and tomatoes were his specialties. When he had a bumper crop of corn, he would bring us corn by the burlap bushel bag full. Way more corn than our little farm family could possibly eat while fresh!

The solution? Freeze it using this delicious recipe. We would get an assembly line going on the picnic table and in no time, we had lots of corn prepped for the freezer.

We would turn a bowl upside down and place it inside a cake pan or sheet pan. Then we'd place each corn cob against the curve of the bowl to steady the cob while you cut the corn off.

It would fall nicely into the pan below. Be sure to scrape the cob well to extract all the juices after removing the kennels. This is called "milking" the corn cob. The corn milk is starchy and sweet. It will help thicken the corn while adding extra flavor to the corn.

---

1. Preheat oven to 350°F.
2. Once you have cut the corn off the cob, enough to make 4 quarts of corn, place in a large pan. Add remaining ingredients and stir to combine.
3. Bake for 1 hour, covered. Stir 2-3 times while baking.
4. Cool and then freeze in quart freezer bags.

4 quarts corn, raw, tipped and scraped
1 cup half and half
¼ cup sugar
1 cup butter, melted

**Tidbits from Jen's Kitchen**
You can leave out the butter and half and half, replacing with 1 quart of water. Heat the corn on the stove top, bringing to a bubble and then simmer for 10 minutes. Cool. Freeze in quart freezer bags.

CANNING AND FREEZING

# RHUBARB SAUCE

*makes 2 quarts*

We had a large rhubarb patch on the farm just at the end of the clothesline. I can't remember how many packages my mom would freeze each year from the patch. It was a lot.

One way that Mom would use rhubarb, either fresh or frozen, was to make a sauce. This simple sauce can be served over ice cream, pound cake or on its own. Mom liked to serve it with a swirl of half and half or heavy cream.

I like it a bit thicker than the way Mom made it, so I reduce the water by about half or even more. I also reduce the sugar by about half as I prefer it to be a little tarter. (When you grow up on a sugar beet farm, the recipes tend to use sugar pretty generously!)

To give it a fresh modern twist, add a teaspoon of lemon zest and a pinch or two of ground nutmeg.

---

1. In a large saucepan, bring rhubarb, water and sugar to a boil.
2. Turn the heat down to medium.
3. Cover and boil gently for 20 minutes.
4. Cool; refrigerate.

**4 cups rhubarb**
**1 ½ cups sugar**
**3 cups water**

CANNING AND FREEZING

# SPICED CRAB APPLE "PICKLES"

This recipe from the Vukku Centennial Cookbook was contributed by May Shelstad. Hjalmar and May were my dad's uncle and aunt and lived on a neighboring farm. I remember visiting them with my parents as a child. Going for a "visit" to another relative or neighbor was one of the social activities of the time, especially in rural areas. As I was just a youngster, I found visiting to be pretty boring.

I must have paid attention at lunchtime because I do remember these crab apple pickles; they were so delightfully different. Sweet, tangy and a bit spicy. Crab apples were one of those farm fruits that were often abundant, but we had a hard time figuring out how to use up the bounty. They are perfect for this recipe.

May's version may not really be "pickled" as the recipe does not include vinegar. Even so, they are a nice change of pace to serve alongside turkey or chicken instead of cranberries. They are also delicious served with a turkey and brie sandwich with arugula and a tad of mustard, possibly my favorite sandwich to throw together.

The original recipe in the church cookbook was simply a list of ingredients with no instructions. We thought you might like a few directions so we outlined the process we used.

---

1. Measure sugar and water into a large saucepan. Stir and bring to a boil. Boil for 10 minutes.
2. Wash and destem apples. Prick the skin of the apples to prevent them from bursting in the boiling water.
3. Put the cloves in a tea ball.
4. Add apples, candies, spices, lemon peel, and the tea ball to the sugar water. Cover and simmer until just tender, about 8-12 minutes. Discard cloves and lemon peel.
5. Pack in freezer safe containers. Freeze.

16 crab apples
1 cup sugar
1 cup water
½ cup Red Hot red cinnamon candies
¼ teaspoon ground ginger
6 whole cloves dash salt
3 strips lemon peels

CANNING AND FREEZING

# ABOUT THE AUTHORS

Jen Switzer is Chief Financial Officer for a healthcare simulation and training company based in Sarasota, Florida. She and her husband, Jamie Switzer, reside in nearby Palmetto, Florida on the Manatee River, where they live on their classic Hatteras motor yacht. Together, they have three children – Megan, Christine and Angela. Jen has also dabbled in the culinary world over the years. She successfully established a personal chef business in Virginia Beach prior to moving to Florida. Her first cookbook, Exclusively for You, Virginia Beach, is a collection of her clients' favorite recipes during her time at the Beach. She has a passion for cooking and baking, which developed from her "Minnesota roots" and growing up on their family farm outside of Breckenridge, Minnesota.

Megan Stezka is an accomplished photographer with roots in Minnesota. She lives in Minneapolis with her partner, Bryce and their doggo, Rocky. They love outdoor adventures with their dog, traveling and seeing live music. In the summer and fall, they forage wild mushrooms and plants. They raise backyard chickens and enjoy tending to their summertime garden. Megan loves cooking with locally-sourced ingredients. If she wasn't in the photography and marketing world, she would love to own a restaurant. Megan's vision for her business is to elevate local entrepreneurs, artists and small businesses in the Minnesota-Wisconsin area with strategic and gorgeous brand photography.

# A SPECIAL THANKS

Special thank you to my parents for answering questions about the recipes and processes as we edited and tested the recipes in this collection. I don't think they figured out what we were really up to but I do think they truly enjoyed reminiscing about the past. They are particularly tickled that their granddaughter, Megan, has become such a wonderful cook, baker and preserver of all things delicious. They have created a heritage founded in love for family and food, a legacy that will be handed down for generations to come.

Big thank you also goes to my sister, Rebecca Bissinger, for pouring through old photos to pick the ones that helped tell the story of our *Minnesota Roots*.

Lastly, to all our friends and family who have helped, encouraged and supported us throughout the process, thank you! Your support means more than you know whether it was editing or proofing recipes in our initial drafts, sampling recipes, or encouraging us along the way.